A Practical Approach to Large-Scale Agile Development

The Agile Software Development Series

Alistair Cockburn and Jim Highsmith, Series Editors

Visit **informit.com/agileseries** for a complete list of available publications.

Agile software development centers on four values, which are identified in the Agile Alliance's Manifesto*:

1. Individuals and interactions over processes and tools
2. Working software over comprehensive documentation
3. Customer collaboration over contract negotiation
4. Responding to change over following a plan

The development of Agile software requires innovation and responsiveness, based on generating and sharing knowledge within a development team and with the customer. Agile software developers draw on the strengths of customers, users, and developers to find just enough process to balance quality and agility.

The books in The Agile Software Development Series focus on sharing the experiences of such Agile developers. Individual books address individual techniques (such as Use Cases), group techniques (such as collaborative decision making), and proven solutions to different problems from a variety of organizational cultures. The result is a core of Agile best practices that will enrich your experiences and improve your work.

* © 2001, Authors of the Agile Manifesto

A PRACTICAL APPROACH TO LARGE-SCALE AGILE DEVELOPMENT

HOW HP TRANSFORMED LASERJET FUTURESMART FIRMWARE

GARY GRUVER
MIKE YOUNG
PAT FULGHUM

✦Addison-Wesley

Upper Saddle River, NJ • Boston • Indianapolis • San Francisco
New York • Toronto • Montreal • London • Munich • Paris • Madrid
Cape Town • Sydney • Tokyo • Singapore • Mexico City

Library of Congress Cataloging-in-Publication Data

Gruver, Gary, 1962-
  A practical approach to large-scale Agile development : how HP transformed laserjet futuresmart firmware / Gary Gruver, Mike Young, Pat Fulghum.
      pages cm
  Includes bibliographical references and index.
  ISBN 978-0-321-82172-0 (pbk. : alk. paper)
  1. Agile software development. 2. HP LaserJet printers.
  3. Computer firmware. 4. Software engineering. I. Young,
  Mike, 1965- II. Fulghum, Pat, 1964- III. Title.
    QA76.76.D47G794 2013
    005.1--dc23
                              2012034286

ISBN-13: 978-0-321-82172-0
ISBN-10: 0-321-82172-6

Text printed in the United States on recycled paper.

Editor-in-Chief
Mark Taub

Executive Editor
Chris Guzikowski

Senior Development Editor
Chris Zahn

Managing Editor
Kristy Hart

Project Editor
Lori Lyons

Copy Editor
Barbara Hacha

Senior Indexer
Cheryl Lenser

Proofreader
Sarah Kearns

Technical Reviewers
Davie Sweis
Lisa Shoop
Robert Bogetti

Editorial Assistant
Olivia Basegio

Cover Designer
Alan Clements

Compositor
Nonie Ratcliff

Dedicated to our amazing wives—Carolyn, Alison, and Tammee.

CONTENTS

FOREWORD

This is the book we've all been waiting for! The Hewlett Packard Laser-Jet FutureSmart Firmware program described in this book—to revamp LaserJet firmware across the entire printer product line—shows how agile fulfills its promised benefits on a large, complex product delivery. Furthermore, the book is written by a team who did it—executive, program manager, and architect—not consultants (like me). The HP FutureSmart Firmware program (multiple products, four-year time frame) succeeded at many levels: It significantly contributed to the future of the LaserJet printer line, it changed an organization's culture, it transformed investment from 95% "get the product out," 5% innovation, to an incredible 40% to innovation (customer differentiation, and so on), reduced development costs by 40%, and reduced cycle time from two months to one day (as they measured cycle time). This program was large (around 400 people), distributed (around the world), complex (firmware, multiple products supported, complete architectural revamp), and fast changing (printer market conditions). This book details the journey that led to these accomplishments.

First, the program changed how HP markets the LaserJet line of printers. The HP web site now describes capabilities such as: transformational innovation, adaptability as businesses change, consistency of applications across printers, centralized management of multiple printers, and the capability to download business applications like a cell phone. The FutureSmart Firmware program delivered on business innovation.

Second, the program changed an organization's culture—not just in development, but over time in product management. In one of the more significant accomplishments, and not an easy one according to the authors, they changed from having each printer product manager impose feature requests for individual products, to a programmatic system synchronized to a firmware delivery train with a program manager who consolidated backlogs and prioritized not just on individual product needs, but on product line needs.

How many organizations decry that they are spending 75% or 80% or even 95% of their development resources on keeping the current system running? They may talk about maintenance and enhancements, but the bottom line is that little is left over to invest in new innovation. That was the case with the firmware system when this program started. They were spending 95% of their resources just keeping up with day-to-day changes, with little left for investing in the future. In my experience, the investment and persistence required to turn these situations around is rare. The FutureSmart team invested in a new architecture, built automated testing and continuous integration infrastructure, and refactored or rewrote code. The authors describe the details of their remarkable turnaround—and the bumps and bruises they got along the way. Not only were they able to turn their investment profile around, they reduced overall development costs by 40% in the process.

There are other organizations who have gone through significant agile turnarounds, but none that I know of whose participants have documented their journey as well for the rest of us to learn from. Gary Gruver, Mike Young, and Pat Fulghum have contributed their journey in a complete and thoughtful way.

Jim Highsmith
Executive Consultant, ThoughtWorks, Venice, Florida

PREFACE

Agile is everywhere. Especially in software development circles, you can't turn around without hearing the term. Agile books. Agile conferences. Agile forums. Dig a bit deeper and all the agile verbiage starts to come out: Scrum, XP, burndown charts. There's even new large-scale agile terms and practices like "Scrum of Scrums" to deal with the complexities of making agile work beyond the typical seven to ten person team. Interesting that something that in name is so "quick to respond" has become quite steeped in theory and process.

This is a story. A story of an experiment about taking agile principles and applying them on a large scale for the re-architecture of a code base and the ongoing innovation and delivery of a multimillion dollar business. A story of listening to what was being said about agile and lean and taking hold of the core principles. But then we needed to look hard at our business situation and use the agile practices that made sense for us, while throwing many renowned agile practices away. We also had to invent new ways of applying agile for our environment because we found they made us more productive. We had to combine basic agile principles with the very real business constraints and the needs we were experiencing. The books and literature described a lot about small, co-located agile teams. Could we really apply agile to more than 400 embedded software (firmware) developers scattered across four states and three continents that reported to four different business units? We needed to completely re-architect a code base with millions of lines of code and a 25-year HP LaserJet Printer legacy of backward-compatibility features to match. We also needed to keep an eye toward a critical future of innovation where firmware was not just the sliver of code to run the hardware, but the complex brains across many devices to enable a new ecosystem of innovation. And all this was occurring in one of the longest economic downturns in U.S. history where our resources were constrained.

This is what drove us to take a leap this large. We had started down the agile path a few times previously (both top-down and bottom-up efforts), all with incremental success. But being hit with so many disruptive forces all at once meant we had to do things significantly differently: to think about improving developer productivity by 10x; to think about putting together an architecture incrementally instead of big-bang; to think about supporting a business model of releasing products not just once, but re-introducing them again and again every quarter with additional innovation; and to think about making quality an everyday, every person, technology-driven concept to fundamentally change the equation of how developers do their job and how long product and feature development cycles need to take.

This is not an academic approach to the problem. This is a practical approach to large-scale agile development based on a four-year experience at HP. It's about how we chose where to focus based on our specific business priorities and needs, and about the missteps we took along the way—and how agile allows and even encourages learning and adjusting as you go. Often the only way to know what works is to find out what doesn't. It's about how our transformation enabled the productivity and agility of a small-team atmosphere within the scale of a large organization, and how it reduced coordination and meeting overhead by putting metrics monitoring at everyone's fingertips so that management could quickly remove roadblocks and keep development on track.

Our hope is that providing this case study will encourage others to start their journey to realizing the dramatic breakthroughs in productivity enabled by agile/lean approaches. It is not a textbook on agile, because lots of those are available. It is intended to be a simple read that can be quickly consumed by busy leaders of large organizations to help them understand what is possible, the potential breadth of the changes, and provide ideas on how to get started. It is also intended to be a catalyst that can easily be shared across an organization considering an agile transformation to get everyone excited about the possibilities and start building momentum for their own personal journey. The book is not about defining the exact right way to do agile, because the agile techniques and approaches are just tools for the real objective, which is transforming your business and improving the effectiveness of your software and firmware development processes. This book lays out what we did and why. It also documents the dramatic improvements in productivity we realized through this transformation. We decreased our development costs per program by about 70% while increasing the capacity for innovation in products and solutions. This was a huge organizational change that provided significant benefits for our business. Our hope is that by sharing this story, you will realize that these breakthroughs are not only possible for your organization, but are probably required to remain competitive moving forward.

This book is also intended for business leaders or aspiring business leaders across industries. Moving forward, software is becoming important not just for technology companies but for every business in terms of how your organization adds value or controls costs. Therefore, having a basic understanding of some leading edge approaches to software development, including the potential impact that technical changes can have on a business, will become more and more important. This book will help show how a fundamentally different approach with a technology can have a dramatic impact not just on the development cost structure but also on the value proposition of a product line.

We start the book (Chapters 1 through 5) by focusing on the foundation of what should drive any agile initiative (especially in a large-scale organization):

- What are the core agile **principles** you want to follow? (Chapter 1)

- What are the **business drivers** you are trying to optimize for in your company? You can make agile work for making your business successful, and not become a slave to it as an end in itself. (Chapter 2)

- How to put in place a strong **architecture** to base everything on—and how to get it in place in an agile way. (Chapters 3 and 4)

- What kind of **culture and management style** do you want to create? This is a powerful part of being successful in large-scale agile. (Chapter 5)

Chapters 6 and 7 then delve into the real nuts and bolts of our processes that enabled us to drive to 10x productivity improvements—continuous integration, automated multilevel qualification, user story definition, and light-touch capacity prediction. We didn't hit any ideal state right out of the gate—we iterated throughout the experience, learning some painful lessons as we went. Agile is just as important in adapting processes as you go as it is in delivering products and features.

The next portion of the book (Chapters 8 to 11) touches on the challenges of making large-scale agile work within a broad, distributed organization, including how to do project management, how to organize teams (pros and cons), and how to work across cultures.

In Chapters 12 to 15, we capture the details of the enterprise-capable tools we used, capture the business results of our agile case study, touch on the new concept called *enterprise agile*, and describe how we interface beyond firmware/software to all other partners in the business. Then we discuss how different our approach was for scaling agile from what is typically done in industry.

Our journey has been very involved and has come a long way; all of this can be very overwhelming to try to roll out all at once, so we end with perhaps the most important chapter of all, Chapter 16, "Taking the First Step"—about how to get started and be successful without trying to solve it all at once.

Although this book contains observations and best practices from our experiences, it also presents ideas for applying the learning to other situations that need productivity improvements with a whole different business case. Come enjoy the journey as we relive it here. Your business is different from ours. Don't get distracted with any perfect practices we'll throw at you (everything's a work in progress here!). But be guided by the power of agile principles applied to your business and its unique personality, opportunities, and constraints.

ACKNOWLEDGMENTS

Although it would be great to list every person who has contributed, that would be impossible. We want to thank every HP FutureSmart Firmware developer, tester, and manager who has made a difference in making this initiative real. Thanks to each of you for your commitment, passion, ideas, and willingness to make this experiment into a broad and successful reality. The concepts and practices and results presented in this book are the result of every person involved in this transformation. It was an amazing journey and we appreciate all your contributions along the way. Without everyone working together and learning from each other, this transformation would not have been possible. THANKS!

We appreciate the support of Von Hansen, our VP and General Manager at HP, in helping to lead this transformation and encouraging this publication. He was instrumental in driving this significant breakthrough for HP and providing us with the support and encouragement we needed along the way. Without his support and initiative, neither the book nor the transformation would have been possible.

We also owe a special thanks to Jim Highsmith for recognizing the value of this manuscript early on and providing the support and encouragement necessary to make it a reality. He helped guide us through the publishing process and helped push to get us the support we needed. Jim also helped get us better linked into the agile community, for which we are very grateful. Without his guidance and support, this book would have never been possible.

We also would like to thank everyone who took to the time to review early versions of this manuscript and provide valuable feedback. It is a better product because of your help. Thanks to Jim Highsmith, Jez Humble, Troy Pearse, Ajay Gupta, Arun Dutta, Keith Moore, Luciano Rocha, Joe Longo, Frank Riskey, Kimon Papahadjopoulos, Steve Townsley, Michael Turner, and Phil Magnuson.

ABOUT THE AUTHORS

When we started this journey, we didn't have much background with agile. We were a team that had a lot of passion around transforming our development processes to improve our effectiveness. We were encouraged by what we read about agile and decided to leverage and apply it to our large-scale embedded firmware development at Hewlett-Packard. What is captured in this story is based on what we found to be effective in transforming our business. In hindsight, it probably would have made sense to read more and better leverage the agile community so we did not have to learn a lot of these lessons through the school of hard knocks. What we found as we got more involved with the agile community as we worked through the publishing process is that much of what we developed was also being implemented by others in the agile community. Because of budgeting constraints, we were not reading extensively or using consultants, so some of the terminology we use is not industry standard. During the review process, we decided that instead of changing all our terminology to match industry standards, we would keep what we developed but insert references to other books where readers could find the latest ideas to help accelerate their journey.

So why did we write this book? We've found that most agile books on the market are written by those who spend their time studying, lecturing, consulting, and writing about best practices from working with different businesses. We thought it might be helpful to publish a book based on how these different agile ideas came together in one company. Therefore, this is our story of turning a large-scale development organization into an agile machine over the past four years. It hasn't always been pretty or easy, but every step along the way has been taken because it worked—in real life. We haven't achieved nirvana, but we've set up a pretty amazing system and environment that works well for us and HP's business needs.

We each have very different roles at HP, and we believe that having someone in each role we've played is critical to the success of an effort like this.

Gary Gruver is formerly the Director of Engineering for HP's LaserJet Core Firmware Lab, and he worked at HP for 22 years. He is currently VP of Release, QA, and Operations at macys.com. Any major initiative needs a true business sponsor—someone who has truly caught the vision of agile, and who can make the business and financial decisions necessary to get huge breakthroughs to happen. Gary has also been able to bring a "manage to metrics" approach that rallies everyone to common measurable objectives without requiring lots of meeting and coordination overhead. Of course, his most critical role is buying lunch during particularly busy sprints for anyone working weekends to finish off key features. His favorite hobbies are cycling and skiing with family (he's married with two daughters).

Mike Young is the program manager directing day-to-day efforts across our many distributed teams at HP's LaserJet Core Firmware Lab. Mike has been involved in development of HP LaserJet Printers for 18 years, and he previously designed satellite control systems for Hughes Aircraft Company. He also is one of the strongest advocates of agile approaches and helped get the organization started down this path before anyone really knew we were doing agile. His hobbies are family (he's married, with two daughters and two sons) and playing racquetball. In agile, we've found that a program manager should spend most of his/her time watching the metrics and quietly coordinating behind-the-scenes to cater to the bottleneck. In our sprint checkpoints, we tend to minimize slideware and maximize problem solving and demos of new user stories.

Pat Fulghum is architect of the HP LaserJet FutureSmart firmware and its development team's agile toolset. Pat's been at HP for 24 years. He found out during the past few years that his favorite escape is scuba diving in Maui with his family (he is married and has a son and a daughter).

A large-scale agile initiative requires a central architect who can help maintain architectural integrity amid many pressures to do otherwise (which keeps the system enabled for the future) and who has the vision for making sure the architecture supports both firmware development and qualification. Pat still loves to get in and dig deep to solve vexing technical challenges. He also loves to find developer productivity improvements (build time, triage time) and has been the passion behind our "10x productivity improvement" vision.

Chapter 1

AGILE PRINCIPLES VERSUS PRACTICES

A recent search for books on agile software development came back with hundreds of hits. Every agile book starts with a discussion of principles in agile, and then very quickly launches into the author's favorite practices. With a title that starts with "a practical approach," you probably guessed correctly that we also talk about plenty of practices. That's because it's tough to roll out a principle to an organization—you can only effectively roll out practices. Practices are tangible, and they involve all the "make it work" things like tools and training and processes. But it's critical to start the conversation with principles. On a recent visit to Bangalore, the software IT capital of India and arguably of the world, we worked with several teams who were faithfully following all the agile practices we had put into place over a three-year period. It was amazing to see what happened as soon as we started explaining the why—the principles. Suddenly, instead of just doing things because "that's the way we do them," the teams started to ask questions and to think about daily activities and how they are done. And they helped come up with better practices for everyone.

This opening chapter describes the fundamental agile principles we started from and how we adapted those to meet our business needs in a large-scale development organization. We end the chapter with a brief comparison of waterfall versus agile development.

The Principles of the Agile Manifesto

The Agile Manifesto (www.agilemanifesto.org, written back in 2001) is amazingly simple and powerful at the same time (see Figure 1.1). It doesn't talk about practices or methodologies. It simply lists some clear principles that can make agile come alive and meet necessary business objectives.

Manifesto for Agile Software Development

We are uncovering better ways of developing
software by doing it and helping others do it.
Through this work we have come to value:

Individuals and interactions over processes and tools
Working software over comprehensive documentation
Customer collaboration over contract negotiation
Responding to change over following a plan

That is, while there is value in the items on
the right, we value the items on the left more.

Kent Beck	James Grenning	Robert C. Martin
Mike Beedle	Jim Highsmith	Steve Mellor
Arie van Bennekum	Andrew Hunt	Ken Schwaber
Alistair Cockburn	Ron Jeffries	Jeff Sutherland
Ward Cunningham	Jon Kern	Dave Thomas
Martin Fowler	Brian Marick	

© 2001, the above authors
this declaration may be freely copied in any form,
but only in its entirety through this notice.

FIGURE 1.1   Manifesto for agile software development

We also highly recommend the "Twelve Principles of Agile Software" that are listed with it (see Appendix A, "Twelve Principles of Agile Software"). But in books and actual application of these principles, the manifesto discussion usually gives way quickly to the long list of do's and don'ts specific to the next great agile find. Don't get us wrong—you'll find plenty of great agile methodologies, practices, and ideas out there. It's just that you can't apply them blindly. Doing everything all at once is too much work and overwhelming. Therefore, you need to think about your biggest pain points and the intent of the different agile practices to determine where you will be getting the biggest bang for your buck.

This book assumes a basic knowledge of agile principles and practices. We do not attempt to provide a broad background on what agile means or what the most common practices are; instead we focus on capturing our experience in applying agile in a large-scale organization. You can check the bibliography for various good books on agile if you'd like to get a basic background. Some of our recommendations are the following:

- *Agile & Iterative Development: A Manager's Guide* (Craig Larman, Addison-Wesley, 2004)

- "Adaptive Leadership: Accelerating Enterprise Agility" (Jim Highsmith, ThoughtWorks, 2011)

- *Continuous Delivery: Reliable Software Releases through Build, Test, and Deployment Automation* (Jez Humble and David Farley, Addison-Wesley, 2011)

- *Scaling Software Agility: Best Practices for Large Enterprises* (Dean Leffingwell, Addison-Wesley, 2007)

Our Take on Agile/Lean Principles

Based on our real-world learning and what we've gleaned from applying the manifesto and other ideas, we've come up with our own top six agile/lean principles. The first two are from lean development, the next three from agile, and the last one is from our own school of hard knocks. We use these to decide whether any new practice or tool is really helping our agile cause or not. It's too easy to get caught up in "everything agile" and forget to look up to see if we're still going in the right direction.

1. **Reduce overhead and waste (keep it simple).**
   If agile practices are adding more overhead to planning and
   development activities than you previously spent on them, then
   it isn't agile. In this case study, the only thing more agile than
   our feature delivery model has been our development process
   and tools. Historically we rolled out major tool/process changes
   only every few years, and we carefully scheduled them between
   major program deliveries. But now we ask questions such as:
   "How can we reduce build time?" "How can we get more integrations and builds per day?" "Why are we still doing that?"
   Analyze daily tasks. Streamline everything. No matter your level
   in the organization, bring it up. Get it changed if it is unnecessary overhead or waste in the system.

2. **Don't overfill your plate.**
   In lean/agile, this is called managing WIP (Work in Process).
   Even after we think we have agile down pat, the moment we take
   our eyes off this principle, deadlines and parallel activities and
   dependencies start piling on, and everyone slows down. One
   manager on our team calls it the "peanut butter approach of
   feature development." As we spread everyone thin across everything, we're guaranteed to lower throughput. *It is counterintuitive, but the more you try to do, the less you get done.* One
   key is to set proper expectations: undercommit, overdeliver.
   We'll talk a lot about this in the chapter on agile planning.
   It can't be done without getting aligned with marketing and
   business leaders, and it involves resetting their expectations
   significantly.

3. **Cater to the bottleneck.**
   It's very easy to expect teams to "just deliver," and to want only
   good news and thus cause bad news to be unspoken until it's too
   late. Is management there to help? Or to drive things harder and
   hope that the bottleneck can come around? Large-scale agile
   deals with very complex projects. There is *always* a bottleneck.
   It is critical to create a culture where the bottleneck is not only
   known, but catered to. Managers look across the system continuously to understand the bottleneck so they can optimize the

system for it. If people know that being the bottleneck gets quick help, they'll let on early and clearly when there's trouble. And in return, they'll be more willing to loan resources in the future to the next bottleneck in the system.

4. **Integrate early and often.**
   We have always had a high quality standard before code changes can be brought to the main code base. But historically we didn't have a simple/automated integration process, so developers would save up large changes before integrating code. Our mantra during our experiment became "commit small functional chunks of code often and test incrementally," rather than holding off and making major changes less frequently. This is one of those fundamental principles that was key to unleashing productivity and quality improvements across the organization.

5. **Planning rhythm.**
   The essence of agile is a planning rhythm. Although we've settled on four weeks (like Scrum espouses) as just right in terms of "long enough to get things done" but "short enough to make it agile," our experience is that the most important thing is to have a regular cadence. During one four-week sprint, we hadn't accomplished what we had wanted, so somehow we decided that we would tack another three weeks onto the sprint so we could accomplish the purpose. The strange thing was, with the additional time we still didn't accomplish what we'd hoped! More time with no fresh objectives just bogged us down. Therefore, we've never changed our rhythm since! We've settled on four-week planning/delivery cycles, where we set up objectives for our whole development organization in terms of what will be accomplished for feature commitment, infrastructure improvements, or endgame for a customer-ready release. In consulting with various reviewers of this book, the general opinion is that you can't really say you're doing agile if your sprints are longer than four weeks. Some have suggested doing two-week sprints, but we've always felt we would incur too much overhead if we tried to re-plan and report every two weeks.

6. **Practitioners should define agile/lean practices.**
   It's so easy to read about and begin to blindly start implementing and following agile practices, or to take hold of a corporate agile initiative and start. Change is hard enough already, but combining that with trying to adopt practices that someone else defined is a recipe for failure. For a process or tool to be most effective, you have to have it defined by someone experiencing the benefits and pains of it end-to-end, every day. It doesn't matter what the experts say it *should* be. Practitioners know what works the best because they feel the daily pain, and because they are constantly asking everyone they work with: "What hurts?" and "What can we do better?"

Figure 1.2 summarizes these agile/lean principles that guide all we do.

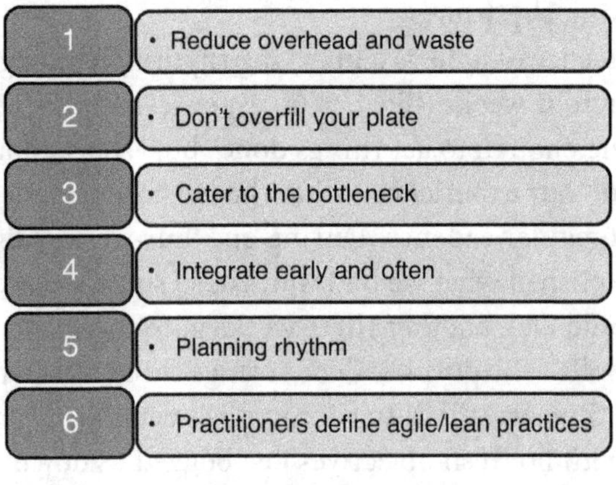

1	• Reduce overhead and waste
2	• Don't overfill your plate
3	• Cater to the bottleneck
4	• Integrate early and often
5	• Planning rhythm
6	• Practitioners define agile/lean practices

FIGURE 1.2   HP FutureSmart FW top six agile principles

A Quick Tutorial: Agile versus Waterfall

Several concepts with agile development provide a major paradigm shift from the traditional waterfall model and are worth pointing out to readers new to agile. The traditional waterfall approach to software development can be broken into four primary phases.

1. An extensive requirements-gathering process where everything about the project is documented in detail so the developers understand clearly what to create and can schedule the work.

2. A detailed planning phase where you commit to features and schedule.

3. The development phase when all the components are developed according to the specification.

4. The final integration and qualification process where all the components are put together and the system is driven to bit release quality.

The founders of agile realized after years of experience with this approach that it had some fundamental flaws. One was that the requirements tended to evolve as the teams learned more during development, and what was thought to be important in the beginning turned out to be less important. Another flaw was that although a lot of up-front work went into determining the schedule in the waterfall model, it was not delivering very reliable schedules. The development, integration, and qualification process tended to be very lengthy and non-deterministic.

The agile approach works to shift this paradigm by addressing some of these fundamental flaws. First, it tends toward "just in time" requirements at the right level of detail. It tends to value working code reviewed with the customer as an approach to embrace the evolving requirements over time. The basic idea here is to start delivering code to the customer with the most important features first that are fine-tuned to meet the customer's needs instead of waiting until everything we thought we needed in the beginning is done. The net result is that the customer sees value much sooner, and through this interaction, some things that were thought to be important in the beginning are never created because over time, we realize they weren't as important as we thought. It is more valuable to deliver the most important features quickly than to take a much longer period of time to deliver everything.

Second, there are lots of changes with agile targeted at addressing the challenges of long integration and qualification cycles. The major shift is to bring the code together frequently and early to make sure it is working well as a system during development. The idea is to make sure at any point the code is close to being ready for release and what is developed has high quality. Instead of having a lengthy integration and qualification cycle, an agile process makes it part of the ongoing development process. This shift is accomplished through approaches like continuous integration/delivery, sprints with complete requirements, test-driven design, and automated testing. All this is put in place so that when customers think they have enough of the capabilities ready, the code is close to being ready to deploy. This is an oversimplification of agile and waterfall, but it is an attempt to frame one of the major paradigm shifts from waterfall development for those new to agile.

Summary

Stick with principles; they serve all of us well. Adapt them to your business needs, and definitely put them into practice and follow your favorite agile methodology. But frequently go back to those principles and confirm you're still aligned with the ones that are critical for your success. Detailed practices and tools can make all the difference in the world, but when implemented and followed blindly, they quickly lead us away from the core principles we started from.

Chapter 2

TUNING AGILE TO YOUR BUSINESS OBJECTIVES

We started with the "why" of agile practices—that is, principles. But there's a deeper "why" that we need to explore. It's really the "why" of the principles you choose to follow. Although agile is a powerful concept, becoming agile just because "it's the thing to do" won't automatically help a business achieve what it is trying to accomplish. To successfully create the significant breakthroughs in your development effectiveness that are possible with agile, it has to be aligned with *why you want to do it* in the first place and *what you need to achieve from it*. You should be agile not just to be agile, but to drive the business results. Start by describing your business situation.

First, sit down and identify your current business realities (where the money and time is going) and strategic objectives (where the money would ideally be spent for your business situation):

- **Cost and cycle-time drivers**
  What are the activities that are consuming your resources and limiting your ability to deliver on time?

- **Value proposition**
  What are your products or services really trying to achieve for the customer?

The final step in establishing the backdrop for an agile transformation and making sure the efforts are tied to your real business needs is to combine the two lists (where are you investing now; where do you need to invest) for a clear view into the problem areas. Use this analysis to *establish clear development objectives* for your organization. *The biggest cost drivers that aren't key to the value proposition are targets for improvements.* If these cost drivers can be architected out of the system, automated, or engineered away, it can free up resources for innovations critical to the value proposition.

The best way to talk about how we tuned agile to our business objectives is to clearly spell out our business situation before our large-scale agile experience began. So in this chapter, we'll give you an overview of HP FutureSmart Firmware that we're using as the case study. We'll identify our costs and cycle-time drivers prior to our agile transformation, explain the value proposition our business needed, and then list the development objectives that came out of our analysis and would effectively close the gap we faced.

Background: HP FutureSmart Firmware Case Study

HP FutureSmart Firmware is the name the business uses to market the latest embedded code used to control LaserJet hardware and enable solutions resident on the device. A typical laser printer consists of the electromechanical print engine, which is controlled by a formatter. The formatter is made up of both electronics and logic. The logic is referred to as *firmware* but can be considered a full-on multitasking operating system. In this case of the firmware for enterprise-class printers and copiers (FutureSmart), it is as complex as the operating system and logic running your PC or laptop or smartphone.

Our business challenges started with a predicament of two-year long development cycles for delivering firmware, and of complex embedded software that had been slowly aging over many years and needed to be re-architected. Big-bang integrations were frequent. Before learning about agile, we had some early improvements and got to the point of 8-week development cycles, a daily build or two, and a nightly smoke test. But even with these significant improvements, some significant inefficiencies existed.

Cost and Cycle-Time Drivers Prior to HP FutureSmart Firmware

The first step is to understand how resources are being deployed and what activities are driving development costs. Honestly assess where software development dollars are spent. It is also important to understand the cycle time for a developer to implement a change and then get feedback on if it works.

Throughout this experience, we've had around 400 developers worldwide needing to get firmware and test changes integrated into a firmware system consisting of several million lines of code, with very high quality expectations. When we started our transition to agile development, we had created a complex environment and code base over many years that took most of our efforts just to keep it going:

- Ten percent of our staffing was for "build bosses" (someone on each team designated as its full-time code integrator) plus a central integration team to accomplish the one or two builds per day we were doing, with many teams doing integration their own way. This was a very manual process of integrating and reverting code, consuming several highly qualified engineers who, as a result, spent very little time actually coding. In this environment, each project team would have a build boss that would gather all the changes by the team every few days and bundle them into a collection of changes. These changes would then be provided to the integration team that would be taking changes from 15 different build bosses for a nightly build with a smoke test. This nightly build would then be provided for additional testing over time.

This approach resulted in a resource sink, but more importantly, it could be up to a week from the time a developer made a change until it got into broader testing on the main code branch to see if it worked.

- Twenty percent of our resources were spent doing detailed planning for future feature commitments that quickly became obsolete or were never delivered. Business and marketing expected a clear "final list of features" one year before product introduction. To provide that commitment, we worked on detailed work breakdowns, schedules, integration plans, and estimates, all of which required constant maintenance and revision, because new discoveries and adjustments are an integral part of any high-tech research and development (R&D) effort.

- Twenty-five percent of our resources were consumed porting the existing codebase and features from one product to another. Because of schedule pressures, we hadn't spent sufficient time to abstract out the code and encapsulate product differences. We also ended up splitting the organization and creating three distinct branches of the previously common code. This meant more focus for each part of the business, but fewer resources for assuring code maintainability.

- Fifteen percent of our development costs were for manual test execution, which was a significant cost driver. Although we had a very large test suite, most of it needed to be executed by technicians, which was a large chunk of the budget. It also meant very long feedback loops from test to development. It was sometimes weeks or even months between when a firmware change was made and when a test actually found an issue. This made for long find/fix cycles, and it consumed a large chunk of the budget. This also meant that we frequently could not add products to our plans because we did not have the resources for testing them.

- Twenty-five percent of development resources were deployed supporting existing products, either fixing customer change requests or making sure we had a consistent set of features across printers and multifunction products (MFPs). With a focus over many years on getting each product to market, we had created multiple code branches that all had to be maintained for the products in the field.

- This left us with limited capacity to focus on the value proposition and customer differentiation that would actually provide the business value needed for continued success.

So that gives a clear picture of where we were allocating our resources. If you add it all up, the firmware development cost drivers were 95% "get the basic product out" and just 5% adding innovation. That is exactly opposite of where the business needed us to be in order to be competitive in the marketplace. So where did we *want* to be spending our money? What was the business asking for? The next section describes our value proposition for making such a substantial change.

Value Proposition of Re-Architecting the HP FutureSmart Firmware and Processes

After establishing where you are spending your resources, it is important to clearly understand the value proposition of your product. Is your primary goal to reduce cost for a given functionality? Is it to release the largest number of products at a given cost? Or is the real opportunity to provide clear differentiation to the customer? Each of these is valid, and there are many more, but the decisions around the trade-offs to make in transitioning your development processes will be dramatically different depending on your specific business value proposition and cost drivers.

To start our agile change, we stepped back and asked what we really wanted to accomplish. What if we could change that "95% turn the crank" reality into something very different with innovation at our core? Following are the real business drivers that we established as our vision and value proposition:

- Our firmware had been on critical path for nearly every product delivered for more than 20 years. We sorely needed to get it off that critical path. How could we *deliver firmware early and often with even higher quality?*

- Because such a large percentage of our resources was spent on the "turn the crank" activities mentioned previously, a significant pent-up market demand existed for more features and innovation. For four years, we tried to spend our way out of the problem, increasing firmware R&D investment dollars by two and a half times across multiple versions of the code base that had split off in an attempt to let each business unit control its own destiny. But it didn't seem to help. We needed to *significantly improve developer productivity and organization agility* to truly lead the market in all desired product attributes and features. We needed to engineer a solution.

- Our business drivers were also changing. Customers had been moving from a previous focus on "buying up to the latest product for faster printing" to needing an *advanced and consistent set of Multi-Function Printer (MFP) features for workflows/solutions* that have the MFP as an integral part. Previously, it had been okay for different products to have different capabilities. But after MFPs became an integral part of their workflows, customers started demanding consistency in the feature set. The technology curve with printers was to the point where the hardware engine speeds and print quality were satisfying customers, and we didn't need to keep ramping up the curve of higher speed or print resolution. More and more product differentiation began originating in firmware. Our firmware had transitioned from a "thin layer of code to help control the print engine" to being more software-like as the critical enabler for supported workflows and solutions. Customers also began to manage their fleet of printing devices, raising the importance of managing devices in a consistent manner.

With these clear cost drivers and opportunities as our backdrop, we were prepared to put agile to work for us (not us for it) and tackle these difficult but critical disconnects in our investment versus value-add picture.

Establish Development Objectives from the Business Analysis

As we started out on our agile journey, we translated this business picture of "where we were spending our money" and "what the business needed" into a clear set of **firmware development objectives** that we felt would close the gap between where we were and where we needed to be. Our goal was that these objectives would help *unleash the product roadmap and enable innovation by reengineering the code and development processes*:

- Create a stable application code base that is always close to ready for release.

- Automate tests and run a full set of regression tests every night.

- Automate the integration process, including autoreverting any code that is not up to par.

- Significantly reduce the work needed to get new products working with high quality and out the door to the market.

- Re-architect to remove product differences, enabling one branch for all products (even refreshes of released products).

- Improve developer productivity by a factor of 10 (build times, streamlined processes).

- Create a common development environment so engineers can easily help across teams.

- Reset expectations and reduce feature estimation activities (commit by delivering).

There was a final consideration in determining how to go forward: Every team or business must not only step back and ask about resource allocation and value-add, but also about the capacity of the organization to absorb change. How much change can the organization handle, how fast, and how many ideas can be driven from your position in the organization? This example involves a large amount of change over a long time period with a big team. Agile transformation can only happen as quickly as your organization has the capacity to invest and is ready to embrace significant change along with that investment. It also matters how influential the thought leaders are in your organization. The final chapter goes much more into the best way to start, but no matter what, make sure you start with the items that will give the biggest bang for the buck and are appropriate for your organizational influence and leverage.

In the following chapters, we will share our experiences and changes that enabled the following results in hopes that it will inspire your organization to start your journey toward transforming your business:

- 2008 to present overall development costs reduced by 40%

- Number of programs under development increased by 140%

- Development costs per program down 78%

- Firmware resources now driving innovation increased by a factor of 8 (from 5% working on new features to 40%)

Summary

What are your business objectives and value proposition? How are you spending your time and resources? What are the pain points you want to overcome? Do your investment areas match your objectives? With our case study as an example, we encourage you to do the same exercise. This will allow you to create a vision for the organization and a roadmap of how to get there. It's easy to get lost in the day-to-day and sprint-to-sprint nature of agile. Having the vision and strategy for where you want to be in the medium or long term is a powerful backdrop to measure all activities against and know if you're being successful.

Chapter 3

ALIGNING ARCHITECTURE WITH BUSINESS OBJECTIVES

As we started out on this agile transformation, we began by investigating what would be the best firmware architecture. We found it extremely important to align code architecture with business objectives and architect the code so that, wherever possible, we could eliminate non-value-added work from the system. The approach to architecture and the directly related approach to coding standards can either lead you in the wrong direction or provide significant breakthroughs in development or deployment efficiencies. Our previous firmware architecture had been formed based on our single-function printer legacy, which, besides being fairly old, was not well suited to the complexities of Multi-Function Products (MFPs).

This chapter outlines the challenges that we faced with our previous aging architecture, the architectural traits we rallied around to align it with our business needs and overcome the previous challenges, and finally how we created a culture to make the new architecture sustainable.

Challenges with Existing Architecture

HP LaserJet Printers have been so successful over the years that keeping up with product schedules while maintaining excellent quality used most of our time and resources. HP is one of the best system integrators in the world, with a strong quality reputation to uphold. As the design and revenue center of our business changed, however, we needed the architecture and processes to change, too. We had made great strides but needed to take another large step forward.

As our architecture aged, we no longer had clean interfaces in the system; so when we changed one area of the code, we had no idea of the impact across the system. Additionally, we had product-specific references throughout, which drove significant inefficiencies into development. Each time we had a new product or small group of products to support, we created a new branch of the code to start the product-specific work (because this overlapped with previous code releases that were still in development and we couldn't afford the new product code turmoil). Because "getting the product done with high quality" was our primary focus, we would do it the quickest way we could—typically adding significantly more product-specific "if/def statements" (if product A, do this; if product B, do that). This meant even more time to port the next release for products C and D. This is a big part of what drove our non-value-added costs of porting the existing code to new products and created a support nightmare (anytime we needed to fix a customer escalation, it required creating the solution, porting the code to 10 different branches from previous product introduction windows, and then qualifying the changes on all those branches).

At the same time, our business had changed from our customer's perspective. When we were developing single-function printers that were passive participants on the network, it was okay to have different features on every product, and the model was to add firmware features to encourage customers to buy the latest products. As HP grew into the MFP market, the device became an active participant on the network in terms of pushing digital content. This brought a new set of requirements in terms of security and authentication so you could track the originator of the content on an enterprise network. With digital sending capabilities, we started getting integrated into our customer's workflow, and all of a sudden it was much more important to have consistent features and implementations across new and older products. Additionally, managing fleets of devices became an opportunity for cost savings for customers.

These new demands in the market were putting strains on our business. The amount of R&D required to support existing products in the field had grown to more than 25% of the R&D budget. We were struggling to keep up with new feature requests from marketing and customers. As mentioned previously, over 4 years we hired many new firmware developers to spend our way out of the problem, but it was not working. We (firmware R&D) were still the constraint in the business in terms of being able to release new products with fully competitive feature sets.

Architecting for the Business: Dynamic Variability and Forward Compatibility

We needed to take a fundamentally different approach. Instead of spending our way out of the problem, *we needed to engineer a solution.* Therefore, as we started bringing up our new architecture, it was clear to the business side that we needed to eliminate all the inefficiencies of having multiple branches and ensure consistent features across the fleet. We really needed one common code main trunk that could support all our new product development along with the existing fleet of current products. To address these challenges, we started with the architecture instead of agile processes because for this type of reengineering effort, the architecture provides the most leverage.

These ideas were radical concepts that brought initial concern to an experienced engineering team during the early development of the architecture. Most of the time, when these concepts were brought up by the Director of Engineering, the engineers would try to ignore it, hoping it would go away and that the director would come to his senses in terms of the realities of developing firmware. Then one day a lead engineer said, "Hey, I think you're right, and here is how we can implement the architecture to meet that objective. We need an architecture with clean, structured interfaces between layers and components. We need to put all the product-specific capabilities in XML files that are referenced throughout the code. We also need an architecture that can be common across all our products for development and testing, with one build that will automatically configure itself at runtime for the specific product." (See Figure 3.1.)

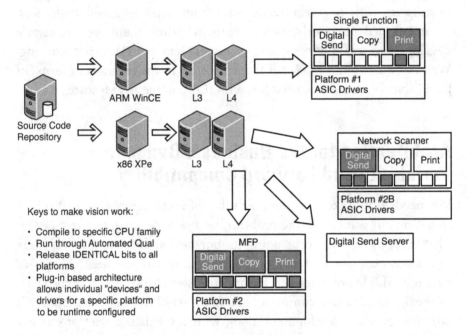

FIGURE 3.1   FutureSmart FW deployment model supporting product variability

This was a huge breakthrough that fundamentally changed the value proposition available for the customer and eliminated large amounts of non-value-added work in the system. The value proposition changed so dramatically that all of a sudden not only could we support releasing products more efficiently, but because it was easy to support all the latest features on the existing products, we changed our plans and set our sights on being able to release a common set of features across the product line with new capabilities coming multiple times a year. This provided investment protection for our customers because the investments made today in hardware would be able to evolve over time with the changing needs of their businesses through future changes in the firmware (see Figure 3.2). *Thus was born the concept and branding of the new HP FutureSmart Firmware.*

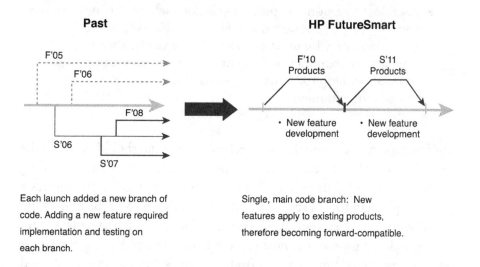

Each launch added a new branch of code. Adding a new feature required implementation and testing on each branch.

Single, main code branch: New features apply to existing products, therefore becoming forward-compatible.

FIGURE 3.2   Investment protection through fleet consistency (industry-leading forward compatibility)

The list of key architectural enablers for FutureSmart firmware we've been discussing is included next. This example shows the leverage an architectural change can have on the value proposition and cost drivers.

Summary of Key Enablers in FutureSmart FW Architecture

- Code identifies hardware it is running on and then configures itself.

- MFP design center (prior architecture was focused on single-function printers; new architecture focused on challenges specific to multifunction products: job queue management, performance, concurrent walk-up/remote user activities).

- Architected around a "feature enable/disable" concept (opportunity to support a whole new business model by making new features available to the whole fleet of devices; for example, a customer buying a device one year and subscribing to future upgrades to keep all HP devices consistent and new).

The leverage you get from the architecture is huge and should be one of the top priorities. The success of the approach requires a good understanding of the market and your potential value proposition, but it also requires a proper understanding of the development cost drivers and the non-value-added work in the system. It shows the value of the management team having a clear vision of the business objectives and providing consistent unwavering focus and drive to find creative solutions. As mentioned earlier, for months most of the engineering community thought the director was crazy until an engineer created an innovative solution to the problem. Then all of a sudden it seemed not only possible, but in some respects intuitive and obvious. And the fundamental characteristics of the architecture became central to all our investment going forward.

Keeping an Architecture Current and Sustainable

After you establish the fundamentals of a new architecture, how can you make sure it doesn't fall into disrepair or obsolescence?

It is critical that someone in the organization who cares deeply about the architecture is given the responsibility and empowerment to be vigilant in checking up on architectural integrity and making sure we aren't violating its basic tenets. We have done this throughout; without it, we would not be nearly as agile as we are today, and the firmware would have some significant problems with scalability across products. When faced with a decision about product support versus architectural integrity, most developers will opt for the quicker way to get the product out the door. At many times in the past few years, we have had conversations (sometimes uncomfortable) about "why did you do it this way?" and "this is how it needs to be done to make sure we can have a business-based scalable architecture into the future." Our reviews of architectural integrity are in part based on code reviews but are also based on tools we built into the development environment to show us when we aren't compliant with the basic tenets of the architecture.

During the development of the new architecture, engineers working quickly to bring up new capabilities would at times take shortcuts and break some of the fundamental tenets of the architecture. Our engineer responsible for defining and ensuring that we delivered to the architectural objectives would find out and take proactive action before the architecture got out of control. Whenever he found the architecture was being compromised, he would purposely make changes that would break the code until it was architecturally correct. We could tell when he had found and plugged a hole because a particular test area would have a huge drop in passing tests or the build would break completely. When this happened, he would frequently get blamed, even though his changes would have been benign if the code had been architecturally correct. It got to the point where we created a new verb from his last name and called it being "Tweded" when this occurred. This new verb is now officially in our urban dictionary. This story is pointed out for a couple of reasons. First, it shows how we were able to have fun while driving improvements. Second, it highlights how important it is for the management team to buy-in to driving the long-term supportability of the code. It would have been very easy to make Roger revert his code when it had a big impact on our metrics. If we had done this, our short-term metrics would have looked better, but we wouldn't have the clean interfaces and fundamentally sound architecture we have today.

It is important to remember that although it is relatively easy to write code, it is very difficult to create a sustainable platform. The natural tendency is to rush a product to market and end up with a mess of code that is difficult or impossible to support. The software industry talks a lot about legacy code that is old spaghetti code (bad architecture without clean interfaces between components), that doesn't have automated unit testing, and is difficult to maintain. It is one of the biggest challenges in software because after the code is written this way, it is hard to go back to clean up the architecture and create the required automated testing. Nobody likes having to deal with legacy code, but it is also important to remember that the natural tendency for a software organization is to create more legacy code by rushing a product to market. One of the most important roles for management is ensuring architectural integrity and sustainability when developing code.

One other critical point: An architecture is never complete. After it initially forms, and the whole organization starts to get involved in dynamically taking it wherever it needs to go, it is critical that the tightest relationships are well aligned with the architecture itself. If teams are organized around the components of the architecture, the firmware will remain as a meaningful asset that enables the future. Otherwise, business pressures and team associations will constantly be at odds with the architecture that a few people will be attempting to maintain. The key to a long-term scalable and robust architecture hinges on making sure things are well aligned. We have invested quite heavily in the technical career path so that the best leaders and influencers in the organization are those most technically competent in each feature and test area. We continue to have a few key architects who watch over the system and assure architectural integrity throughout.

Summary

An architecture will drive productivity, for good or for bad, for many years. It is critical that it aligns with your business objectives. In our case, the architectural approach has had a significant impact on our business, one in which we support a large number of products with embedded firmware. For different businesses such as software, the questions used to evaluate the architecture may be very different. For example, although development cost drivers will still be important, deployment and operational cost drivers will probably be more important. Is your architecture designed for flexibility if you are going into a new and evolving market? The architecture is going to be difficult to evolve when you get too far down the path, so it is important up front to make sure it has been evaluated against your business objectives and cost drivers. Then, establish whatever it takes to maintain that architecture through the pressures of tight schedules and the natural divergence of a broad engineering organization. Create standards, tools to enforce them easily, and organize to make sure that the architecture maintains its integrity.

Chapter 4

How to Establish a New Architecture Using Agile Concepts

As we've described, our journey to agile started with completely redoing the firmware architecture of our large-scale firmware system that had evolved over the years as it powered HP LaserJet Printers and MFPs for more than two decades. The previous architecture successfully supported dozens of award-winning products but was architected for single-function printers and was past its prime in terms of enabling the future innovation needed for success in the new business realities.

As we embarked on the architectural effort, we reflected back on previous architectural initiatives we'd been involved in and decided we needed to take a radically different approach to avoid some major pitfalls. In this chapter, we discuss how we began the move into agile development by using the architectural effort itself to establish our agile rhythm. We then describe key practices we used to maximize the progress and drive cultural shifts in the organization.

Re-Architecting Iteratively

Most re-architecture efforts start with a period of 6 months or more of not having anything to test. Then, by the time the system is up and running well enough to try it out, there's so much new, unproven code in place that it's impossible to ever catch up with testing—not to mention that it's too late to redo the architecture if we guessed wrong and it didn't optimize the system around the points we had hoped.

We brainstormed how to bring up the architecture differently than we had previously. We decided that 4-week steps would be the right amount of time to get something meaningful done (that we could demonstrate) but still short enough to provide time for course corrections as needed. We adopted an iterative model and started proving out feasibility. So interestingly, it was our early architecture effort that propelled us to agile.

A Note on Our Agile Cycles or Mini-Milestones (MMs)

We started our agile activities before reading about many existing methodologies. Although in hindsight what we do is quite like Scrum, and MMs are really just agile sprints, we've never fully adopted all the standard terminology because we had already invented our own. We recently completed Mini-Milestone 50 (50), meaning it's now been just over 4 1/2 years since we started this journey (each MM is 4 weeks, and there are 12 per year). That gives us 4 weeks a year of "bonus" time so we can feel like there's at least an occasional break from the endgame-like nature of agile cycles. The whole idea of MMs came as we tried to figure out how to start showing progress with the re-architecture effort.

Making Progress

After many informal discussions between several architects on what the system might look like (driven by the business objectives discussed in the previous chapter), Pat, our lead architect, kicked off prototype teams and spent all day for several weeks reviewing the results of each prototype and providing guidance to the team. He sat at his desk all day, and every half hour a different small group of engineers would come by to review their work and plan the next steps. The first six Mini-Milestones (MMs) of our whole experience were specifically about reviewing their work and planning next steps. The key concepts that stood out in this foundational process were the following:

- One strong architect needs to be responsible for looking across the entire system, driving plans, approaches, and decisions. It's also helpful if the architect is a great implementer. An architecture isn't proven until it's implemented. It is important to have an architect who is willing to get into the code and get his or her hands dirty. The architect must understand the difficulties and provide code that addresses the most technically challenging issues.

- By having several small prototype teams reviewing progress frequently, the organization was able to be brought along in terms of feeling ownership for the success of the architecture and believing in it. The whole re-architecture effort brought about more holistic learning and moved faster as a result of so much interaction/review. The quick prototypes also allowed us to quickly review progress and adjust to things that weren't working. Dead ends on the prototypes could be thrown away because the issues were discovered before a significant amount of code was developed.

- Having a single overall reviewer meant sharing learning across groups and also having a greater understanding of how it would all work together. It was a great process for getting the organization up to speed quickly on the new architecture. Fast and agile. It was also a great process for the central architect to learn everything possible about how the new architecture was working and where adjustments were required to make the entire system work.

- Progress was shown through prototyping different "thin slices" of end-to-end capability. Getting something up and going to learn from and adjust before developing a significant amount of code was very successful. It allowed us to figure out quickly what wasn't working before there were large investments in each aspect of the architecture. We would demo new thin slices every four weeks, and this effort went on for two years until all the aspects of the architecture had been proven out.

The Thin-Slice Model

Figure 4.1 is a diagram of the agile process we used for making this happen. It shows how we started with the simplest thin slice we could create through the system to make sure there was working code to validate the architecture as soon as possible. This was typically just the happy path, but it showed how all the components were plugged together.

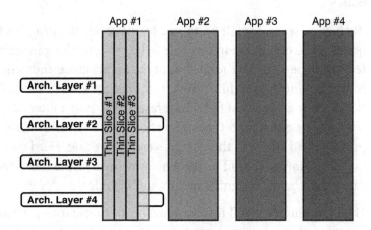

FIGURE 4.1   Thin-slice approach to bringing up a new architecture (at startup)

The next step was filling out the first application with more capabilities and resolving the constraints and issues encountered off the happy path. After that, it moved on to additional applications, and through the process, the architecture was finalized and filled out, as shown in Figure 4.2.

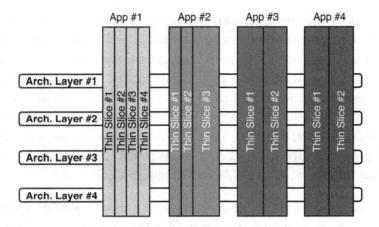

FIGURE 4.2   Thin-slice approach to new architecture (finish)

Figure 4.3 shows the general model of how we iterated through each architectural slice. Reviews and prototypes were critical to the success of this venture, followed by the constant evolution of incremental improvements to get the whole system right.

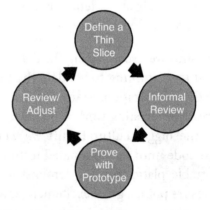

FIGURE 4.3   Agile architecture process

Creating Cultural Shifts Through Architectural Demos

In our Mini-Milestone checkpoints at the end of each four-week cycle (sprint), we had the involved engineers demo the prototype of a thin slice that made it in time. The overall program manager (or Scrum-Master, who makes sure the teams live by the agile principles and who organizes the sprint reviews/checkpoints) would get the developers excited about demonstrating a thin slice with working code at each checkpoint. This would get the engineers driving for a clear deadline where they wanted to show off their work. It also gave the broader organization an opportunity to start seeing real progress. We used these demonstrations during the checkpoints as part of our change management process where we were shifting the culture to an agile development model.

The first cultural shift we starting making was asking developers to be sure the demonstration was of working code fully integrated onto the main branch. At first, developers would use our traditional approach of wanting to show some code they had been fine-tuning on their development box right up until the last moment. After we started specifically asking at each demonstration whether it was integrated code, the engineers knew the development box approach was not going to work. This resulted in some failed demonstrations because someone brought code in the night before that broke a demo or two, but it started the right cultural shift to the agile development model of continuous integration.

The second cultural shift we drove during the demonstration was asking to see the automated tests running to validate the functionality. At first this was a shock to the organization. Many felt that testing was someone else's job, and the really interesting work was showing the working code. This was probably the bigger cultural shift we were driving, because working code is just code until the automated testing is in place to make it part of a supportable platform. The demonstrations at checkpoints provided specific closure points, great excitement about small but critical progress, and an opportunity to start driving the required organizational changes. It may feel a bit strange having a bunch of managers sitting around reviewing a simple demonstration early on, but we would recommend not overlooking the value of this process in your sprint checkpoints.

Summary

Most architectural efforts happen on the side without full integration into agile tools and processes. There may be prototyping going on, but it isn't typically until several months into the architectural work that things start coming together enough to integrate and test as a system. The thin-slice-based agile approach we took ended up not only achieving a much stronger/cleaner architecture, but also moved us forward with the real-world practice of agile principles much more quickly and effectively. It set the foundation for the years following as we went beyond the basic architecture framework to involve everyone in agile practices for all product and feature work.

Chapter 5

THE REAL SECRET TO SUCCESS IN LARGE-SCALE AGILE

So, we have a business plan. We have a great architecture. And we have the agile principles squarely in our sights. In Chapters 6 and 7, we'll get into the nuts and bolts of the day-to-day agile development machine (the continuous integration capabilities and quality systems, and the stream-lined planning focused on maximizing throughput vs. optimizing pre-dictability). But first we want to describe the hardest and most impor-tant part: how to make large-scale agile real. To roll it out, do we take a top-down approach? Or bottom-up? We've tried both on their own quite unsuccessfully. The top-down approach was first tried several years ago—kind of a "mandated agile." We started with the metrics and tried hard to drive the organization to respond. We definitely achieved some business results from it, and it was the first time we recognized the power of monitoring and reducing Work in Process (WIP). But in a "mandated agile," we could never rally the troops because it was "do this because we said so" versus "do this because you understand the value." In a large organization, the other extreme is a bunch of engineers who understand agile and believe in it, but never can get traction either without sponsor-ship. It doesn't just "come together" without some sort of purposeful gov-ernance in place with management. So what's the best way to get there? How can you create an agile system that integrates all these concepts and hums along, responding quickly with high quality to whatever features or products or innovations come next?

It's all about the people, and about how we manage. It is about coordinating the work of a large number of people to deliver working code. It is about learning from the organization what is working and what needs to change so you can make agile adjustments to your plans and approaches to continually improve productivity. We are strong Scrum-adopters from this perspective. As Craig Larman says about Scrum in *Agile and Iterative Management: A Manager's Guide*, "Process is only a second-order effect. The unique people, their feelings and qualities, are more influential" (p. 2). Everything we do is to build up people, to get them excited about what we deliver (and how), and to help them know that it really is all about them.

To make large-scale agile work, it's also important to have the fewest number of people required to accomplish the business objectives. This helps drive the productivity focus. The firmware architecture naturally resembles the organization chart and drives discussions and documentation of the interfaces. Therefore, the smaller the number of people involved, the simpler the architecture and the less time involved defining the interfaces between developers because they are managing more code internal to their component.

Change for People's Sake

It's all about how change management is handled (steady on the rudder but constant pressure on the vision). A key part of an agile management approach is spending time with the developers to understand what is working and what isn't. They need to understand that the management team is there to help with their struggles and change things to make the processes more efficient. That's why we drive productivity changes. That's why we constantly ask "what waste do you see that we can get rid of?" And that's why we cater to the engineers with tools and processes. Historically, the embedded firmware groups in our organization have been process heavy. There were many policies and procedures that everyone needed to follow. They adjusted slowly over time (major process changes only occurred in between major program delivery, every year or two), and the changes were primarily focused on increasing system quality rather than thinking of the productivity impact of the organization. It's not that our agile processes today aren't about quality. Many of them are, but when we roll them out, we first talk with developers and make sure it isn't complicating their lives or putting in unnecessary overhead. We strongly encourage developers and testers to come back with ideas to streamline things, and we often implement them immediately. We constantly ask, "How can we reduce build time? Integration time? Test triage time?" One of our initial mantras was "10x developer productivity improvement." After many challenges along the way, based on our chosen measurements of "build time," "test/triage time," and "integration time," we've actually achieved it! Details on our tools and processes are captured in Chapter 6, "Continuous Integration and Quality Systems," Chapter 7, "Taming the Planning Beast," and Chapter 12, "The Right Tools: Quantum Leaps in Productivity."

The other critical piece of the "change for people's sake" idea is fundamentally how people are treated through the challenges of change. This applies not only to developers and testers but also to partners in the business. Our relationship with the product owners in marketing has also been critical to nurture and work as close collaborators as we've managed such high change in expectations and process (more on this in Chapter 7). Aside from anything "agile," we have adopted an approach of trusting and respecting everyone through whatever situation arises. And we approach everything optimistically. Going agile, especially large-scale agile, requires creativity and innovation—almost like being an entrepreneur. One of the qualities of a successful entrepreneur is being an optimist. Risk-taking entrepreneurs often generate the innovations that drive businesses forward. The leaders of this whole initiative (upper management, key architects, program management) have perhaps been a bit idealistic at times, but definitely always followed and enacted a strong vision. If we had gone forth with more realism, we never would have tried stretching for those innovations that have been key to our success.

Metrics Are a Conversation Starter

It's also all about how you respond to pressure and bad news. Historically, we had a culture where no one would speak up if they weren't going to hit a schedule or were struggling with solving a difficult technical problem. Have you ever heard of "schedule chicken"? It was alive and well with us! No one wanted to be the bad guy, which means we learned about problem areas late, and there were a lot of burned-out, lonely people trying to get off the critical path but rarely succeeding. Our managers work closely with the teams to understand how much work they can handle and when. Many organizations use consultants and agile coaches for this, but we've always relied on our own managers (we've focused on training all our managers on the agile principles we promote and let them work the details with their teams). This requires good tools for tracking real-time what is and isn't getting done. The key, though, is *not to manage by metrics but to use the metrics to understand where to have conversations about what is not getting done.* Always trust that engineers are doing the best they know how or can in the situation. People want to do a good job; so when the work is not coming along, there is usually some key reason: a need for training or technical help, a need to improve architecture or processes, or there is just too much work in the system and you are going to have to adjust priorities to make progress on that particular vector. Having clear, integrated priorities for all work makes a big difference, especially when you give the message: "If you're working on something at the top of the priority list, you have access to anyone, anytime to get whatever help you need."

The worst thing that can happen with metrics is that people start feeling beat up, which means they will start hiding data. If the management team does not understand the constraints because of the team's concerns about getting beat up for not being on time, then you never know where to help or how to move resources around. If teams see management as helping to move resources and provide creative and helpful changes, the issues will be made visible early, and you can respond and adjust in real-time. This leads to a positive reinforcing cycle that is key to the agile management approach.

At the most stressful times of development and deadlines, we've had several friendly competitions with balloons placed with "the team with the most issues/change requests," and so on. This has helped turn stress into a more enjoyable process. Most people enjoy "delivering innovation" more than the endgame of a release, but when it is a game or a friendly competition, everything gets closed out more efficiently and people have fun along the way.

Iterative Model of Agile Management

We came up with a model we call the Iterative Model of Agile Management (see Figure 5.1). Agile at its best is not just a development model but a way to manage people and processes. It shows that management doesn't "know it all" and is willing to listen, adjust, and change for the betterment of everything, with more focus on real people and what they care about. This model is all about setting new objectives for the whole organization every four weeks, and then putting metrics in place to track how we're doing against those objectives. Those metrics are then used continuously, not to drive people harder, but to have a conversation to discover where the problem areas are and what we can do to help. Then we learn from it and adjust whatever is needed for the next cycle.

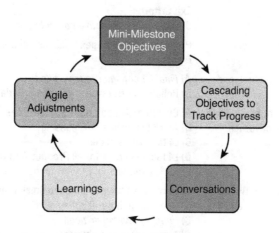

FIGURE 5.1   Iterative approach to agile management

Mini-Milestone Objectives

We start each monthly Mini-Milestone (sprint) with a clear set of objectives and high-level priorities for the organization. The idea here is to set aggressive goals the team feels are possible and important to achieve in 4 weeks. It is surprising how much you learn in a month and have to adjust based on discovery during development. We typically drive hard for these stretch goals but usually end up hitting around 80% of what we thought we could at the beginning of the month. During the Mini-Milestones we don't track team-based or program-level burndown charts, but we do track progress. We had some teams try burndown charts, and we looked at it for the overall program but felt the overhead for tracking accuracy was taking capacity away from maximizing throughput. Instead, we have an overall set of metrics we track during the MM that helps align everyone in the organization and gives us a clear view of where we are not meeting the objectives. The objectives include user stories we implement and qualify but also other initiatives including early hardware support, endgame activities, and tool/process improvements (whatever's important or urgent to the business becomes an objective). Table 5.1 is an actual list of prioritized objectives for our MM30 sprint (2½ years into our agile experience).

TABLE 5.1   Sample Mini-Milestone Objectives (MM30 Objectives)

Rank	Theme	Exit Criteria: Objective Met/*Objective not met*
0	Quality threshold	P1 issues open < 1week L2 test failure 24-hour response
1	Quarterly bit release	A) *Final P1 change requests fixed* B) Reliability error rate at release criteria
2	New platform stability and test coverage	A) Customer Acceptance Test 100% passing B) All L2 test pillars 98% passing C) L4 test pillars in place D) L4 test coverage for all Product Turn On requirements E) 100% execution of L4 tests on new products
3	Product Turn On dependencies and key features	A) Print for an hour at speed to finisher with stapling B) Copy for an hour *at speed* C) *Enable powersave mode* D) Manufacturing nightly test suite execution E) Common Test Library support for four-line control panel display

| 4 | Build for next-gen products | *A) End-to-end system build on new processor* *B) High-level performance analysis on new processor* |
| 5 | Fleet integration plan | Align on content and schedule for "slivers" of end-to-end agile test with system test lab |

Cascading Objectives to Track Progress

The fact that these metrics and prioritized MM objectives are online and available for everyone does a great job of aligning the organization. The metrics at the overall program level are a summation of the metrics for each section manager and project manager. Therefore, everyone in the organization has an aligned set of goals to strive for and track each month. These metrics range from the status of requirements development to change requests to tests passing. The tools even enable us to track individual code contributions throughout the day or summary metrics for different time periods. The ability to track this information and have it online has basically eliminated tracking and status meetings. We don't require scrum meetings or scrum of scrum meetings to know what's going on. Within an hour of reviewing the metrics in the morning, it is easy for the management team to know more about the status of the program than we ever thought possible. In fact, it got to the point where the developers nicknamed the Director of Engineering "the unblinking eye" because he never misses anything and always knows what is going on in the organization. At the same time, he spends very little time in meetings getting status or tracking progress. The nickname started one day when the Director noticed that someone broke the build 15 minutes after it happened. He stopped by the engineer's desk to see what happened and the engineer promptly responded, "What are you, the unblinking eye? Don't you miss anything?" This led to a great April Fool's joke where the entire floor was decorated in the *Lord of the Rings* theme. There were bloodshot-eye balloons, name plates we changed with the theme, and the online build environment icons were even changed. It may seem silly, but it really helped to make it a fun environment where you wanted to work when you knew it was safe to make fun of the Director of Engineering.

We send out an automated daily early morning email with a summary of the objectives and the metrics, with a link to get to an hourly version of the same data online. We've included samples of some of the key metrics we track in Figure 5.2. (Each cell in the tables is a drill-down to the details through each layer of the organization.) These all help us make sure we're both maintaining the appropriate code stability and making appropriate progress in each sprint. We go into more detail on the meaning and purpose behind these metrics in later chapters.

Open Change Requests

Section Manager	P1 Punch list	P1	P2	Newly Found	Newly Fixed
Section A	0	2	20	2	2
Section B	0	0	3	0	0
Section C	3	14	29	0	2
Section D	0	5	6	0	1
Section E	0	4	52	4	1
Section F	3	14	25	1	2
Total	6	39	135	5	8

Requirements Status (current sprint)

Section Manager	Not Started	Under Dev	Implemented	Under Test	Verified	Total
Section A	5	3	0	0	4	12
Section B	14	20	5	27	12	78
Section C	3	7	0	4	4	18
Section D	8	10	1	0	15	34
Section E	11	11	6	19	10	57
Section F	17	20	9	6	22	74
Total	58	71	21	56	67	273

System Test Execution [test runs are "out of date" after a week (auto) or a month (manual); drill-down shows breakdown by team]

Product	Simulator Auto Pass/Exec	Emulator Auto Pass/Exec	Product HW		
			Auto Pass/Exec	Manual Pass/Exec	Out of Date Exec
Product A	15288/16114 (95%)	2132/2352 (91%)	10/10 (100%)	390/411 (95%)	141
Product B	8251/9262 (89%)	359/589 (61%)	2/17 (12%)	107/132 (81%)	20
Product C	5577/6113 (91%)	224/1035 (22%)	1/4 (25%)	155/167 (93%)	46

Integration Queue / Automated Builds Status

Daily Summary Metrics for 05/24/2011

Builder Type	Build Type	Builds Processed	Builds Passed	Builds Failed	Branches Processed	Branches Passed	Branches Failed
⊞ Stage 2 Builder	Stage2 Combined	10	4 (40%)	6 (60%)	133	105 (79%)	28 (21%)
⊞ Stage 1 Builder	Stage1 CEQbar	36	31 (86%)	5 (14%)	36	31 (86%)	5 (14%)
⊞ Stage 1 Builder	Stage1 Qbar	50	42 (84%)	8 (16%)	50	42 (84%)	8 (16%)
⊞ Stage 1 Builder	Stage1 XPQbar	23	21 (91%)	2 (9%)	23	21 (91%)	2 (9%)
Totals for all Stage 2 builds		10	9 (90%)	1 (10%)	133	105 (79%)	28 (21%)
Totals for all Stage 1 builds		109	94 (86%)	15 (14%)	109	94 (86%)	15 (14%)

FIGURE 5.2   Sample metrics for prompting daily conversations

Conversations

The majority of the time is spent having conversations to understand where and why we are not meeting objectives. If you are going to use the flexibility of agile principles to improve the effectiveness of your organization, you must constantly be seeking to understand what is working and what can be improved. *You can't manage by metrics and only drive to meet the numbers. The metrics help you understand where to go to have conversations about what is and isn't working.* People want to do a good job and are doing their best, so when they are not meeting a clear objective that they felt was achievable at the beginning of the month, it's important to understand why and what needs to be adjusted so you can help. You also need to be careful with how the management team uses this new detailed view into the development process. The engineering director frequently knows within an hour when someone has made a big mistake and broken main. It is very easy with this visibility to create a destructive, blame-type culture where everyone slows down to the point of trying to make everything perfect before committing, which would kill productivity. At the same time, if there are repeat offenders, it should lead to conversations to reset expectations. A lot of this happens through peer pressure when people are bringing in code that is impacting the productivity of the engineers, but management does need to play a role (although carefully) because knowing so much can be used to drive the wrong behavior.

Learning

One example of what we learned from this iterative approach to agile management is that the management team also needs to make sure it is using the tracking data to help understand where to move and adjust resources. During the development process, we try to actively advertise the bottleneck for the program. This helps the organization understand that if there are general tasks, like test failure triage where another team can help out, that a non-bottleneck, non-critical-path team should step in to lead the initial investigation. The broader organization should also look at loaning developers to the bottleneck and adjusting other resources to help. If you can create this culture and really help out when needed, it makes everyone feel that they are on the same team. It's suddenly not such a bad thing to be the bottleneck, because the organization is there for support. When we used this process the past few years in our development, the bottleneck shifted several times, based on helping out and teams rallying to get caught up. The credibility earned by the management team by providing this help can lead to a positive reinforcing culture where teams that got off the bottleneck remember how great it was to get help while they were stuck, and then they naturally step up to help others later.

Agile Adjustments

The iterative part of agile management involves setting specific prioritized objectives at the beginning of each sprint (or Mini-Milestone) and tracking progress throughout the Mini-Milestone (MM). It involves learning and adjusting during the MM. Then it involves taking what was learned and accomplished during the sprint to set the objectives for the next MM. Sometimes those objectives start with the 20% that was not accomplished during the last MM, but frequently it contains significant changes in objectives to improve productivity based on what was learned during the previous development cycle. We've found that this objective-setting process for each sprint is far and away the best way to control Work in Process (WIP) and get the full benefits of lean development. It focuses the organization on what is really needed, and makes sure we don't keep trying to do too much and thus become less efficient and slow down throughput.

Summary

This "real secret to success" has carried us through so many challenges these past four years as we've rolled out large-scale agile in our organization. Focus on the people. Find joy in interactions. Listen. Learn together. And at the end of the day, don't forget the importance of the phrase: "Metrics are a conversation starter." Recognize the tendency to manage to metrics. Then stop, take a deep breath, and start having those conversations. HP's founders, Bill and Dave, came up with a management style they called "Management by Wandering Around" (MBWA) that completely focuses on the people. That has become a somewhat lost art in today's HP. But using real-time metrics to trigger the right conversations has brought back MBWA to our organization in a big way.

Chapter 6

CONTINUOUS INTEGRATION AND QUALITY SYSTEMS

Our first thought was to split up this chapter because we have a lot of concepts/examples to cover. However, the more we thought about it, we decided there's absolutely no way to split it up. Continuous integration and quality are everything together, and nothing without each other. The first half of this chapter describes what we did to make continuous integration work for us—it was definitely an iterative process! We started out very simply before ending up with a full autorevert system, which means catching major failures/issues in new code during a staged integration/test process so that the change never makes it onto main if it breaks anything. The autorevert system was dramatically more efficient and powerful. The second half of the chapter describes the quality system we have evolved to that is tied in directly with the continuous integration system. Both of these are critical fundamentals of making large-scale agile work well. We end the chapter with a summary of our productivity results that have come out of our automated delivery pipeline, and we discuss some considerations for applying CI and automated testing to enterprise software systems.

Reducing Build Resources and Build Time: Continuous Integration

As mentioned earlier, integration was a fairly painful process for us before we started looking into continuous integration techniques and tools. With the architectural limitations we had previously, our integration process had become challenging to the point that each team carved out a role we called "build boss," who was the code integrator for that team, so the individual developers didn't have to get involved in getting their code into the main code base. The build bosses did nothing else but get all their team's code changes working together, then submitted them as an integration request. A separate central "integration team" created the overall firmware build by merging the changes from each build boss into the main code trunk. This was a very manual process, and a code change from a developer typically took a whole week to get fully integrated into the system if everything went well. If something went wrong, it was back to the beginning of the queue and required another week of manual integration activity. Besides the high overhead of this process in both people and time, it caused two other issues. First, without intending to, we were encouraging developers to integrate infrequently with large code changes (use large batch sizes; the antithesis of lean development). Second, we were causing very slow find/fix feedback loops. Yes, developers could find their own coding issues via unit tests before committing their code (although at the time, unit tests were not our focus), but any integration or system-level issues weren't found until the developer was off working on the next feature. This task-switching and latency of finding code issues made for very inefficient development and low feature throughput rates.

So we started studying Continuous Integration (CI). We definitely weren't industry leaders at this point. There were already many books on Extreme Programming (XP) and other agile methodologies utilizing CI. But with approximately 400 firmware developers needing to get code changes integrated on a firmware system that was several million lines of code in size, we were definitely on the large/complex side of anyone attempting to roll out CI. All the agile literature said that "small, co-located teams" were the key to success. But we didn't have that luxury; not only did we have a very large development group, but we also were spread across four states and three countries around the world.

We found a great starter article on CI by Martin Fowler written in 2006: http://martinfowler.com/articles/continuousIntegration.html. This article encouraged keeping things simple to start with, so we did (we were a little more complex than "grab the turkey when it's your turn to integrate," but not much more involved). One of the fundamental premises of CI is that "frequent small builds are best." The goal of these small builds and associated automated testing is to find any coding problems that need to be fixed as quickly as possible. The key to this objective when processing as many code changes as we are is to get a full build with as much testing as possible on the smallest number of changes. Our goal is to be able to quickly identify any significant change in main stability (tests passing) down to a specific commit that can be reverted or quickly fixed.

We tried multiple Source Code Management (SCM) systems over a few years before landing on GIT, an open-source SCM that handles complex code integrations easily and well—a real key to successful continuous integration. We created a simple automated integration and build system utilizing CruiseControl (an open-source basic continuous integration tool) that kicked off on a time interval (about every hour) and built the system with whatever commits were in the queue at the time. Any developer could submit code changes at any time as long as the build was green. If a new build was in progress and you submitted changes, it was considered risky but was still often done. If the build was currently failing, it was considered a misdemeanor to commit a change set (I don't think anyone ever got arrested, but piling on top of an existing pile of failures to unwind was never appreciated). The automated build system also ran a small automated integration test suite we called "qbar," which stands for "quality bar," on the grouping of the hour's worth of code changes. Integration time is a combination of how long the central build takes plus the time it takes to run the centralized smoke test. Whenever this process worked, we succeeded in dropping our integration time from a week down to an hour! This was tremendous, and it really did speed up the feature throughput and timely test feedback. This was fundamental to changing our processes over to agile.

If the build plus qbar test ever failed, any engineer who had a pending commit in that batch had to go join a virtual chat room so that together, the developers in that commit could figure out the problem and who needed to revert their code changes. Although it was only a misdemeanor to commit on a red build, it was considered a felony to "commit and run" (meaning commit your code changes and not stick around until the build was successful, because you were required to be in the chat room if it failed). This drove many people to wait and commit late in the evening because the build would usually break a few times a day—normally during peak commit times.

One of the metrics we use to determine overall productivity and throughput is how many firmware builds we can produce in a day. When we started CI, each time a fail happened, it was at least a couple of hours before the system got back on its feet again. We often had multiple failures during the day, which basically ate up half the normal daytime workday, so we often would only get 5 to 8 builds a day (still much better than our 1 to 2 builds a day in our previous very manual system). We created a metrics page we called the "red/green show" that showed hour-by-hour when the integration system was up and ready to accept new commits. Too often the red/green show was a sea of red during normal working hours (see Figure 6.1).

Even though we preached the concept of integrating small changes early and often, this initial continuous integration process actually was a disincentive for developers to commit changes regularly because they could do everything right and still get caught up in a failure because of intermittence in the system or a stupid mistake by someone else. Our goal was 80% uptime each day, which we actually achieved fairly often after a while, but the problem is that during the busy times of the day (9 a.m. to 5 p.m.), it was only up around 50% of the time.

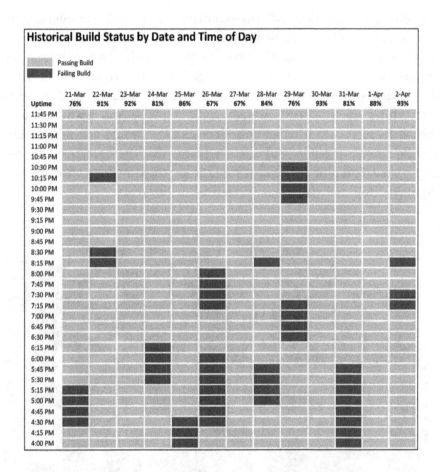

FIGURE 6.1   Red/green show (build uptime; first-gen CI toolset)

There were many late-night chat room sessions going on, and integration was still a frustrating experience. Luckily, we had several people with a great sense of humor that made it almost fun to be in the chat room working through the integration failures, but a person can stand only so much fun at 1:00 a.m.!

It got to the point as the code base grew and we worked to increase the coverage of testing in qbar that we would more and more frequently get not only "an integration test fails every time," but would see intermittent test failures regularly due to some test/code interaction. As these made it into the system, it would destroy the productivity and morale of the engineers. When an intermittent issue got into the system, an individual developer could either root cause the issue or try again to see if it passed and went green. We started calling this "L1 craps" because it was a random roll of the dice as to whether your code changes would get in each time you integrated. It got so bad at some points that the developers created and posted a graphic in the chat room to get the director's attention (see Figure 6.2, and yes, that's Gary's picture, the director).

FIGURE 6.2   "L1 craps" (intermittent failures)

After 18 months of this painful CI process, we knew something needed to change. When things went smoothly, we were enjoying the efficiencies of up to 20 builds a day, but when bad code made it to main, it killed our productivity. We were struggling to find the right balance between keeping main stable and enabling code to quickly make it to main to support our productivity objectives. It came to a head one week when a bunch of intermittent code or tests had made it onto main, fully opening up a game of L1 craps. The director was picking on the build team to get the intermittency out of the system, and they were getting tired of chasing a moving target. They finally raised the test coverage in qbar to the point that, with the intermittency in the system, nothing was making it to main all week. Several frustrated discussions occurred between the director and the build team over this point. The build team felt it had put up a good barrier to stability so main didn't get any worse. The director pointed out that while no new code was getting in, it would not get any worse; but it also would never get any better. He felt what we really needed was a process to let all the good code in but keep all the bad code out. The response from the build team was "well, duh!" Easy for the director to say, but it would be very difficult for them to implement. Then about two weeks later they came back with a new system.

From this, we created a new integration system called *Integration Queuing (IQ)*. It's a home-grown integration tool that consists of two stages. IQ Stage 1 is a developer's personal commit. It gets submitted and run in a central test farm. Every developer has his or her own stage 1, and each starts executing real-time as a developer commits their changes. Each is processed and, if successful, gets promoted as part of a group to IQ Stage 2. If unsuccessful, the change is automatically reverted and the developer is notified—all without impacting anyone else committing code. Figure 6.3 shows an example of the developer commits in process in Stage 1 and Stage 2.

The primary goal of Stage 1 integration is to keep stupid mistakes from hurting others so that the good code can make it in more frequently. This accomplishes the ideal case of autorejecting any code causing test failures before it gets to the main code trunk.

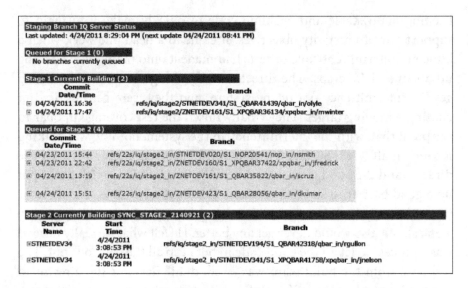

FIGURE 6.3 "In process" developer commits in IQ

Stage 2 then kicks off on a time interval with any commits that have made it past Stage 1 successfully and processes these code commits all together, running a similar test suite to the one in Stage 1, but with more extensive testing where possible and on multiple platforms, including some hardware (but still automated). If any merge conflicts occur that cause any test failures, the whole set of commits in a given IQ Stage 2 get autoreverted. This gets the train wreck off the tracks so traffic can flow (the next IQ Stage 2 group of changes) and just the few affected have to do the extra work of recommitting. *This approach has created a process that enables large-scale continuous integration without ever having main broken* (see Figure 6.4).

We ended up choosing this model because it provided the right balance of real-time quality versus feature throughput. A combination of "my personal change looked fine" (Stage 1) along with "a small group of changes created a successful central build" (Stage 2) gave flexibility and quality without overwhelming the system. The integration success rate has gone up dramatically as a result of this improvement. We are now consistently at 12 to 15 good builds a day. They've slowed down to every couple of hours each, but the percentage of success and the lower frustration levels—and the fact that people can "commit and run" all they want at their favorite time of day—has been so worth it. We've also invested in integration tracking tools to see the current status and estimated time remaining of every commit in Stage 1 or Stage 2, which has made it possible for managers and testers to track and know when fixes and features are coming. There is also a tool to track which tests are failing for all the builds, so if an intermittent issue makes it into the system, it is easy to see and track.

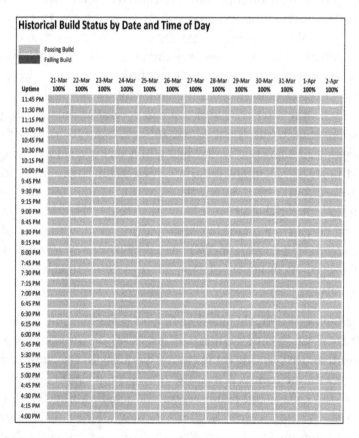

FIGURE 6.4   Red/green show after rolling out IQ

In consulting with various reviewers in getting ready to publish this book, we've found that modern off-the-shelf CI tools can help achieve similar benefits with a feature called "pre-tested commit," "preflight build," or "personal build." This practice is discussed in detail in a book by Jez Humble and David Farley, titled *Continuous Delivery*. To this point we have described technically how our CI process works, but we have not spent much time covering the behavioral changes that were part of the process. As we started down this path, we would continually hear that it would be fine for little changes or small features, but what would happen with really big changes or features? CI obviously would not work for that! For big changes with multiple components, we would need to develop a different process. This was the mindset going into this transition and a big part of the organizational resistance. What we found was the opposite. After four years of a major re-architecture effort with significant changes, we can only think of two or three times when we made a conscious effort to hold other things off while we brought in a major change. Each time after we did it, we had several of our lead engineers pointing out that it wasn't necessary. In fact, it got to being a point of pride where lead engineers would bring in a major change through our standard processes. It might require testing a few components together offline before committing, or a little extra testing up front to reduce the risk, but then major changes would come through the queue along with everything else. When you think about it, this was not that big of a risk because it could get automatically reverted or manually reverted or fixed later if it caused major issues with the full regression suite, but it was a big cultural shift.

Now, for the most part, the developers have made the cultural shift and commit their latest code to main at least two or three times a week. Whatever they are working on is always synced with the latest code. The feature may not be complete and the testing might not be in place, but as long as the code is not being executed (including unit tests), there is no harm having it on main. The idea is to have all the collaborators for a new feature committing their changes to main on a regular basis (via the IQ system). Then, when everything is ready, we start running the system testing and validation on main instead of on a separate feature branch. This is a very different mindset and approach, but we have found it works well and takes a lot of complexity out of the development process.

Achieving High Quality with CI: Automated Multilevel Testing

After we architected to make it easier to turn on a product, we went in assuming that if we also invested in automated testing to reduce the cost drivers for qualification, we would be successful. But as the architectural prototypes started coming together and getting checked into the SCM system, we realized quickly that CI was not possible without a rock-solid quality system with quick feedback. The system will be successful only when the infrastructure and tools are rich enough and robust enough to enable the vision of getting code and tests rapidly into the code main trunk. We needed a system that would quickly and efficiently let the good code in but also automatically keep out as much bad code as possible.

So after we got basic CI going with IQ, the next thing we did was to establish a model of ever-increasing testing over time. We established levels of testing, L0 through L4, based on when the tests are run and how many tests are run. All levels of testing include both unit-level developer tests and functional system tests. As we move up the levels, we also add in various nonfunctional testing areas, including performance, reliability, and memory testing. We used three stages of testing:

1. Integration Testing (levels L0 and L1)

2. Stability Testing (levels L2 and L3)

3. Regression Testing (level L4)

Each level consists of both unit-level tests and system-level tests. A big push (that was not natural or easy to start with) has been to make sure we have the right harnesses and tools in place for developers to be able to focus on unit testing as a part of their everyday work. We started with a culture where testing was primarily a system-level activity done by the test developers, not the feature developers. Finding the right balance has been critical; it is still a work in progress and a cultural change.

We run our highest value tests the most frequently. Integration Testing (L0/L1) has the highest value tests and Stability Testing (L2/L3) has the next highest value tests. We use test passing metrics to drive behavior for L2/L3 and L4. We manage stability by ensuring that the L2/L3 tests pass at 98% or higher. We manage the L4 test pass rate to ensure that we don't accumulate too much quality debt that will keep us from being able to quickly release the code at the end of each quarterly release. In discussions with Jez Humble (one of the authors of *Continuous Delivery*), he discusses a similar concept in his book. Instead of calling it multilevel automated testing, he calls it "deployment pipeline implementation."

Figure 6.5 shows how our IQ system (L1 testing) integrates with the other levels of automated testing (L2 through L4). It has become a fully integrated system, flowing naturally from the developer's individual commits in L1 Stage 1, to grouping them into small batches in L2 Stage 2, then running different test sets at different frequencies per day to assure our code quality is maintained.

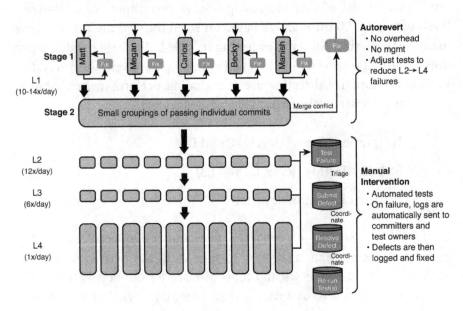

FIGURE 6.5   Continuous integration and test system

Figure 6.6 gives a quick summary of the definitions of the levels of testing. In the following sections, we describe in detail the timing and the types and purposes of tests in each level.

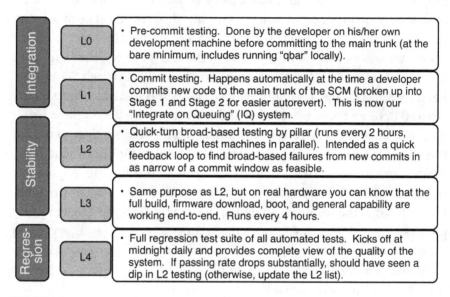

Integration

L0
- Pre-commit testing. Done by the developer on his/her own development machine before committing to the main trunk (at the bare minimum, includes running "qbar" locally).

L1
- Commit testing. Happens automatically at the time a developer commits new code to the main trunk of the SCM (broken up into Stage 1 and Stage 2 for easier autorevert). This is now our "Integrate on Queuing" (IQ) system.

Stability

L2
- Quick-turn broad-based testing by pillar (runs every 2 hours, across multiple test machines in parallel). Intended as a quick feedback loop to find broad-based failures from new commits in as narrow of a commit window as feasible.

L3
- Same purpose as L2, but on real hardware you can know that the full build, firmware download, boot, and general capability are working end-to-end. Runs every 4 hours.

Regres-sion

L4
- Full regression test suite of all automated tests. Kicks off at midnight daily and provides complete view of the quality of the system. If passing rate drops substantially, should have seen a dip in L2 testing (otherwise, update the L2 list).

FIGURE 6.6   FutureSmart FW testing levels

L0 Testing

This testing consists at the very least of running a common short smoke test to make sure a developer doesn't break the system in a major way. Then they execute their individual unit tests for the components they are changing, and often a team-specific short suite of tests. It is *not* intended that L0 testing become so big as to guarantee that all the post-commit testing levels will all pass 100% of the time. This would drive integration cycle times up so high that "frequent small integrations" that are fundamental to Continuous Integration (CI) would never be possible. L0 is all about engineering judgment. About what is "just enough" testing to avoid wreaking havoc on the overall system, but still allowing developer productivity to remain high.

L1 Testing

L1 testing has evolved a great deal over time, as described earlier in this chapter. It is key to overall productivity as well as how many firmware builds we can produce in a day. The big difference between L1 and the remaining testing levels (L2 through L4) is the difference between autorevert versus manual intervention (refer to Figure 6.5, the right side). By design, we don't "stop the current train" for L2 through L4 testing. For those levels, the test fails and we have mechanisms (auto-email, reports) to be aware of what failed and why, so we can get on these issues quickly and get tests passing again. It has finally become clear to us that this autorevert process at L1 is a huge breakthrough for our productivity! Besides architecting correctly to drive business results, this is probably the next biggest fulcrum point. Anything that makes it on to the main trunk thrashes the whole organization in terms of tracking and analyzing progress, test failures, tracking change requests, and so on. Everyone in the organization gets involved in that thrash. If you autorevert, especially in smaller groups (ideally one person), you focus the effort to the one place it makes the most sense.

Autoreverting is fast and efficient, automatic, and it doesn't require status or planning meetings. In the same way that metrics alignment can take status meetings out of the process, autorevert can take huge amounts of work out of the system. When bad code makes it to L2 testing or beyond, responding to failures all becomes manual.

L2 Testing

This form of testing is kicked off on a timer every two hours and uses the last good firmware build from L1 testing. If you can't autorevert in L1 testing, the next best option is to have as many builds a day go through L2 testing as possible so you can quickly catch and address the offending code. L2 tests (frequent high-level test coverage per pillar) are intended to be the protection mechanism of L4 (daily full regression per pillar). If we see a failure in L2 tests that we can act on quickly, it prevents us from seeing a large spike in failed L4 tests that night. L2 is designed to make sure nothing catastrophic was missed in L1 before we get a full day and 100 commits down the road to have to debug after L4.

Each pillar of the firmware system (print, copy, fax, scan, security, extensibility, and so on) is allotted one test machine in the farm for a maximum of two hours of tests—whatever they feel is the best subset of their full L4 regression suite. By design, it should be a somewhat dynamic test suite. As new features are added, coverage in L2 should be provided. As certain areas become completely stable and L2 never finds any issues, those tests can be pulled out (if over the two-hour limit). Two hours was picked to get quick response back on a failure.

We put a mechanism in place we call Test Delta Emails (TDEs) that go out to all developers who committed changes in a particular build that goes into L2 testing. The email goes out only if a test that was previously passing now begins to fail. The email includes the name of the test, a drill-down to the details of the failure, and a zip file with everything required to replicate the test on a development box. It's amazing how the walls between developers and testers melt away when developers automatically have everything they need to re-create the failure. The L2 TDE process is a lot like the old L1 chat room process, except that it's not going away. Although a manual response is required (vs. autorevert for L1), it quickly gives us significant test coverage (12 times per day), and most of the failures get fixed (or the change reverted) within a day without even bothering to submit a change request to track. One of the primary measures of success for the effectiveness of the L2 suites is that we notice a failure in an L2 suite before a spike of failures hits our L4 testing (that runs every 24 hours).

L3 Testing

L3 testing is just like L2 except on emulator hardware, which runs every four hours. Because HP FutureSmart Firmware runs embedded on hardware, at some point we have to make sure that something beyond our simulation environment actually works (although we continue investing in the simulator substantially so we can continue developing most features and finding most code issues there). If L3 goes down, our test partners (software, hardware, system testing) can't get new firmware, so it becomes urgent to get fixed. This happens often enough (every few weeks) that we need to put in place the next iterative improvement to either get hardware into L1 or provide duplicate hardware so that if a hardware problem exists, we can try it out on a backup unit.

L4 Testing

This testing is quite amazing to think about—running the whole regression test suite every night, when it used to take six weeks. L4 failures aren't necessarily urgent to fix unless we're getting close to a release candidate to be shipped out to the customer. They are prioritized based on how many tests a particular issue is blocking. But the real beauty is, we know our quality within 24 hours of any fix going into the system. You can imagine that it is a lot more helpful for the developers to hear that what they committed yesterday broke something, rather than to hear that a test is broken based on something somebody did sometime since this test was run six weeks ago. And we can test broadly even for small last-minute fixes to ensure a bug fix doesn't cause unexpected failures. Or we can afford to bring in new features well after we declare "functionality complete"—or in extreme cases, even after we declare a release candidate. Now that's agile!

Continuous Improvement of the Deployment Pipeline

We also use these different levels/purposes of testing to find and remove waste from the system (become more lean). Here are a few examples in our testing practices that have helped us remove waste:

- Our practice of considering any issue not found by L0 through L4 testing (usually by exploratory testing or test partners) as a "test escape." We work hard to close these holes and find the issues in less expensive ways.

- Analyzing all issues found after we branch the code to prepare to deliver the quarterly release out to customers (the final weeks of "endgame" of the release). Why didn't we find them earlier and cheaper?

- Continually updating the L2 test suite to ensure it is the most effective use of the two hours. If the L4 test passing rates drop significantly when the L2 tests are still passing fine, you know you have a big hole in the L2 test suite that needs to be plugged.

Productivity Results of Our Automated Delivery Pipeline

Can you see now why we combined CI and our quality system in the same chapter? *CI without a solid quality system is a recipe for disaster.* Just because we can commit more frequently doesn't mean we have a better system unless we're also efficiently driving the right autorevert level and the most efficient manual intervention levels of maintaining quality as well.

The results for what we've accomplished with all this have gone far beyond our expectations. Figure 6.7 shows a daily summary of the throughput we are now achieving. Previously, we were bringing in 12 to 15 changes per day (about 10,000 lines of code change), our integration processes manually produced one or two builds per day with only daytime support and all manual reverts, and to run through all our regression testing took six weeks (we had a handful of automated tests that ran every night). This is a great indicator of developer productivity as well. It looks like we met our "10x improvement" in going from 15 to 150 changes a day, from 10k lines of code to 100k lines of code integrated per day, from 2 to 14 system level builds per day, and full regression testing formerly taking six weeks going down to one day. And there are still plenty of things to focus on, including measuring and increasing our test coverage, making sure any "test escapes" (problems found by our test partners or in the field) all have automated tests put in place, and making our test development and triage more efficient. (Chapter 12 talks about our Common Test Framework and how it has evolved to help with this.)

Figure 6.7 is a summary of what happens on a typical day in our system—the number of changes submitted by developers, the lines of code changed, the number of builds, and the number of tests and test hours. That's a lot of throughput!

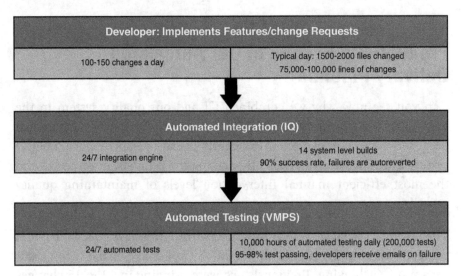

FIGURE 6.7   HP FutureSmart FW development results (daily)

Sometimes we step back and ask, "Is this even humanly possible?" "How does it all just work?" "We shouldn't be able to integrate that much code that quickly."

But the amazing thing is that continuous integration and large-scale agile development works with the right quality system. We're watching it work almost seamlessly every day. We would never go back to where we were. The business now has certain expectations of what can happen that would never allow us to return to where we were before. And our previous process wasn't nearly as fun! But remember that just like all things agile, this is a work in progress. Who knows where we'll be in another two or three years. It should be a blast getting there, though!

Special Considerations for Enterprise Software Systems

In this chapter, we showed how all the changes in CI and test automation provided breakthroughs in our productivity. It also provides a systematic enterprise-level solution for ensuring the fundamental agile paradigm of always having the code base stable and ready for release. This requires carefully thinking through your deployment pipeline and the stages of automated testing. Although it would be nice to be able to run every test on every commitment one at a time, in practice, it is not practical when you have a large number of developers and a large number of automated tests. Therefore, you have to think carefully about how you build out your deployment pipeline, including which test you run where and where you turn the build red or autorevert versus tracking test passing rates. The basic principles you need to keep in mind are that you are trying to keep the system always close to releasable by integrating the entire system frequently while isolating the issues in the code to the fewest number of possible offenders.

In this example, we detailed how we built up our code and tests for an embedded FW system that runs on a printer. The basic concepts apply to any large SW/FW system, but for an enterprise SW system there are additional principles for consideration. For example, most big Enterprise SW solutions require a large database, which can be difficult to load for multiple builds a day. Consider creating a test database or having your automated tests written so that they create the data required for the test. The previously referenced book, *Continuous Delivery*, has some great guidance for how to address a deployment pipeline with databases. The other special consideration with large SW systems is how the different software applications build into an enterprise system. When you are building a deployment pipeline, the goal is to keep the system stable and to isolate any defect to the smallest number of people quickly so it can be fixed or autoreverted.

Enterprise software systems, which typically have different applications running on different servers—some of which may be using waterfall development methodologies—require special consideration. First is where to use red builds or ideally autorevert. Is this done for each component multiple times a day, and if so, how often are you integrating and testing the entire system? If you are using a test database, how often do you test against the production data? Also for enterprise systems, you can't always test the entire system because it could create unacceptable results, such as preshipping actual products. Therefore, you are going to have to create tests harnesses somewhere in the system. In our case, we created a test harness to replicate the behavior of the mechanical print engine so we could automate a large number of tests on a rack of blade servers. Creating a test harness is a fairly labor-intensive process of maintaining code that will never ship in the product and should be avoided if possible. However, test harnesses can be extremely valuable for isolating less-stable portions of your enterprise software system from the CI process.

For example, if you have several software applications that need to work together that are all investing in CI and automated testing using agile approaches, you probably want to avoid the investments in test harnesses. This can be done by starting your deployment process and autorevert of each application in isolation using unit tests. Next, run system tests on new components of each application against the latest known good application versions that are part of the agile development process. At this step, you can autorevert the latest version of the application that broke the system tests. After each of the new application versions is passing all the system tests against known good versions, you can integrate all the newest application versions to catch any merge issues. Using this process, you will be integrating the latest components frequently while isolating issues to individual applications and the least number of committers, all while avoiding any investments in test harnesses.

In a large enterprise, however, there may still be applications in the system that are using waterfall development approaches and are not investing in CI or automated testing. In these cases, it can be extremely valuable to invest in test harnesses to isolate your CI process from instability in those components. It is still important to integrate frequently with those applications to discover any issues with the interface and test harness, but you don't have that instability causing false failures in the deployment pipeline. In fact, when you know all the tests are passing with the latest versions on the agile applications and test harness, the agile process has in essence created a large-scale test automation system for the waterfall components! Just take the latest known good components and run the same tests with the test harness removed. This enables frequent integrations of the entire enterprise SW system with both agile and waterfall applications, which will help address a big challenge for most large enterprises that are still transitioning from the waterfall development model.

Summary

This chapter reviewed how we put together our automated testing process with CI to create dramatic breakthroughs in development productivity. It is fundamental to the agile paradigm of always having the code close to release quality. We covered how we created integration queues and autorevert processes to make this smooth and efficient. This approach was related to our experience with embedded firmware development, so we also highlighted special consideration for deployment pipelines for enterprise software. This included some breakthrough ideas for bridging the gap between applications using agile and waterfall development methodologies.

It is important to understand and design your deployment pipeline up front. Where are you going to turn your build red or ideally insert your autorevert process? How are you going to stage your automated testing? How often are you going to integrate the entire system? Where does it make sense to use test harnesses, if anywhere? These are all great questions, and there are probably more. This chapter provided a good overview, including how it worked for us. Before you start your journey, we would highly recommend your thought leaders read *Continuous Delivery*, by Jez Humble and David Farley, so you can avoid our school of hard knocks.

Chapter 7

Taming the Planning Beast

In Chapter 1, one of the six key principles we introduced as fundamental to our success was "don't overfill your plate." The single most important thing we've done to keep this from happening is to completely overhaul the way we do planning and scheduling. We like to think of planning/scheduling/estimating as a "necessary evil." As you already know based on your reading so far, we focus all our energy and efforts on increasing feature throughput (with high quality, of course). Well, planning/estimating by its nature doesn't increase feature throughput, it reduces it. It happens because the organization wants predictability. A productive part of planning is making sure we have a clear architecture and feature roadmap and definition, but for the "scheduling/estimating" part of planning, the only reason to do it is to assure the business has what it needs to make financial and investment commitments. *Every hour we spend planning a feature is an hour we don't spend delivering it (the real goal).*

It wasn't easy, but we have completely changed the expectations of management and marketing as to what is needed for a commitment. We have also tamed the wild beast of up-front planning that was previously taking 20% of our resources. Because of the planning horizon of products, and a standard product life cycle that all product programs followed, we were committing to a final feature list 12 months in advance that we could never deliver due to all the plan changes over that time. Our planning resources were the same as the development resources, so they would stop working on features to do detailed work breakdowns and scheduling. This model meant we were always in a "locked in" mode where we had to say no to any late-breaking requests that came up (or throw all our "plans" out the window). It meant that everyone would work crazy hours for months at a time to meet our commitments, because the estimates were always inaccurate (as they always will be). It also meant that firmware continued to be the critical path for getting products to market and caused regular late and painful discussions with marketing and the program teams on "here are all the features you're now messaging that you aren't really getting."

The first difference in our planning approach now is that with a common code base that is architected for scalability, and with a highly automated and simple integration and qualification system, we can separate out "get a hardware product out the door" from "deliver a set of features on that product." Turning out a new hardware product goes much more smoothly and is now done much earlier than before. With quarterly releases, the products pick which release train they need to get on to support the schedule. If they don't believe they have a rich enough feature set, they wait for the next release, but they can go out the door on time from a firmware dependency viewpoint. Any slip is due to their own hardware schedule or, occasionally, their wait-for-more-features choice.

For our new-wave, light-touch agile planning in a large-scale environment, we've invested in the following:

- Tools for very **light-touch predicting** of how far we'll get on a "1 to N" feature list (without delving into the details or even engaging the development resources much) such as ballparking and trend watching. These prediction tools are explained in the next section.

- Prioritize everything. Then allow priorities to self-drive the organization. Establish expectations that whenever needed, anyone drops what they're doing and helps the person with the higher ranked user story (requirement or feature) or change request.

- Full-time system engineers who do **just-in-time feature definition** using user stories with marketing and feature requestors to offload the developers and give them a clear path forward when they're ready to engage.

In doing so, we've gone from almost all of our developers/managers spending 20% of their time planning to having a dedicated 2% of our engineering staff (system engineers) doing up-front work that helps streamline development (other technical leads still get involved in the user story reviews, but we're still at no more than 5% of the organization involved in this phase). This is explained in detail later in this chapter in the section "Just-in-Time User Story Definition." We've seen this role called "business analyst" in the wider literature, but we prefer the system engineer term because we believe this role can be best filled by someone with an R&D background who can communicate more deeply with the developer and tester community (and still be focused on working with marketing and others requesting new features).

The chapter ends with a discussion about convincing the business that agile planning is okay.

Predict by Ballparking and Trend Watching

Even without doing long-term detailed planning, there's clearly still a need to evaluate incoming requests and have some idea of the organizational capacity for feature delivery. Why do *you* do planning? It's critical to have a clear intent for any planning process. Planning of large software/firmware development efforts can be very labor intensive and can create plans that are hard to maintain and quickly obsolete. Is it to be used so the business can be sure the development team is aggressively signing up for stretch goals? Is it to scope resource requirements to plan hiring? Are resources and scope fixed so it is a matter of projecting schedules for messaging and revenue projections? Is it to coordinate components to ensure maximum throughput?

Ballpark Prediction: R&D Early Response to High-Level Initiatives

Before anyone ever requests a new specific "feature," there are large initiatives that are being pushed by the business. Just like "new product support," we have to be able to give some answer to these initiatives so those business teams can know how to move ahead. Instead of what we historically had done with a full feature list and work breakdown of every feature, we began doing a high-level analysis approach (very high-level estimates to get approval/alignment on the project, but no detailed plan of how to get there or even the detailed specifications). Twice a year, we create a simple spreadsheet (see Figure 7.1) showing the capacity of each major group in the organization. We have our system engineers do a 10-minute estimate of engineering months of effort for each team for each initiative, and with almost no involvement from the development teams, we had an accurate enough picture that Initiatives 1 through 9 were fine. But after that we would either have to hire or move resources around, or we would not have the capacity to deliver for some collaborators. This prompted very healthy discussion and seemed to meet the business need without breaking the bank using resources to do the detailed plans. In fact, we didn't even slow down development. It also doubled as an investment portfolio analysis to see if we needed to move people between teams. We always have our top architects review all initiatives as well to see if any technology limitations/constraints exist that would be major blockers. It's okay to be surprised by smaller technical issues, but we need high-level alignment and review.

Trend Watching: Quick Response to All Feature Requestors (Where They're Likely to Land)

One of our goals is to inspire confidence in the rest of the broader organization: product marketing, technical marketing, R&D partners, and business leaders. The very idea of agile planning makes them a bit nervous because they don't know when they'll get a new feature delivered. To offset this, we strive to optimize the request process around efficiently getting back with the requestor to make sure our technology roadmaps and plans are aligned with the request and that it's in the right place on the 1-N list. We've found that, even with feature requests from actual customer escalations, it's far more important to quickly acknowledge the request than it is to quickly deliver it or even commit to a specific release. But if we leave the requestors hanging for weeks or months, they get disgruntled, they disengage, they try to do an end run to get what they want, and our working relationships and trust suffer.

Rank	Initiative	High-Level Estimate – FW Engineering Months												
		Component 1 (25-30)	Component 2 (20-25)	Component 3 (30-40)	Component 4 (30-40)	Component 5 (20-30)	Component 6 (20-30)	Component 7 (20-30)	Component 8 (15-25)	Component 10 (40-50)	Component 11 (20-30)	Component 12 (20-30)	Other teams	TOTAL
1	Initiative A		21				5	3		1				30
2	Initiative B	3							4				17	24
3	Initiative C		5							2	1	1		9
4	Initiative D							10		2	2	2		16
5	Initiative E				20							3	5	28
6	Initiative F	23							5	6			2	36
7	Initiative G									2				2
8	Initiative H										5			5
9	Initiative I												3	3
10	Initiative J		20	27			17			39	17	21	9	150
11	Initiative K		3	30			3		3	14			12	65
12	Initiative L									2				2
13	Initiative M	3						10		6	6	6		31
		29	25	51	30	20	25	23	12	74	26	38	59	401

FIGURE 7.1   Spr11 1-N high-level risk/resource analysis

So we came up with a method for predicting based on where a feature is on the 1-N list, without doing any planning on that feature whatsoever. Given that our resources were constrained in the down economy for extended periods of time, it did not make much sense for us to design a system that would show the need for hiring, so the intent of our planning process was to maximize throughput and ensure we were working through the requirements in priority order. We went to a 4-week time slice approach with our sprints (MMs) and tried to work toward user story (feature) granularity that was between two and four weeks of an engineer's time. This enabled us to track how many user stories are delivered in each sprint. From this, it's possible to project about where we'll get in the 1-N list (the "Input Queue"), but of course we avoid committing to anything too low on the list.

We simply look at our Input Queue relative to the size of our sprint-to-sprint delivery, and do a projection. As you can see in Figure 7.2, we haven't exactly maintained a steady-state feature throughput level. In getting the full architecture in place, we were doing yearly instead of quarterly releases for the first few years, and as a result we had multiple sprints for final qualification. We now believe we're finally getting back to a steady-state throughput (two sprints of delivering 40 to 50 user stories each, followed by a final qualification sprint with only limited user story delivery for the next release). We just recently analyzed the latest 1-N list with product marketing. You can see, based on the number of user stories in the Input Queue, that it should take us about two quarterly releases to deliver the 191 current requests (80–100 per release). New requests may come in, but we will place them where marketing wants them in the 1-N list and deliver accordingly. We also monitor this to assure our teams aren't biting off more than they have typically been able to deliver (increased WIP = decreased throughput).

Over time, we do expect feature throughput per sprint to go up as we get more efficient in our processes (driving waste out of the system), create more capability in our engineers, and get into the second and third generations of a new architecture. We're now striving to find the right balance to get back to a reasonable steady-state throughput level that will keep the organization focused and impassioned but avoid burnout.

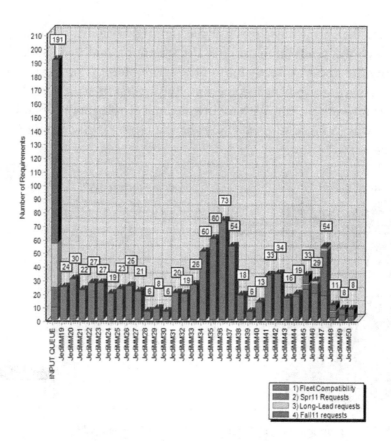

FIGURE 7.2   FutureSmart FW user stories per sprint

Clear Prioritization

One of our mantras is to minimize meetings and allow work to just happen. The thing that enables this to work is incredibly clear prioritization. We start with prioritizing the sprint objectives. If a person has to help deliver two sprint objectives, there's never a doubt where the effort should go if a resource conflict arises. We sacrifice lower-ranked objectives anytime it's needed. We don't actually list any sprint objectives that we don't believe we can accomplish going in, but because new task discovery and adjusted delivery dates are a standard part of any development process, we optimize around the higher-ranked objectives.

Because the sprint objectives are the top high-visibility priorities, and there's always plenty more work in the system beyond that (but at lower priority if it doesn't directly impact the sprint objectives), we also prioritize every requirement that comes into the system to make sure the most important work is clear. We have invested in key roles in the organization to allow us to make sure we always have a clean 1-N list (Input Queue) [see Figure 7.3].

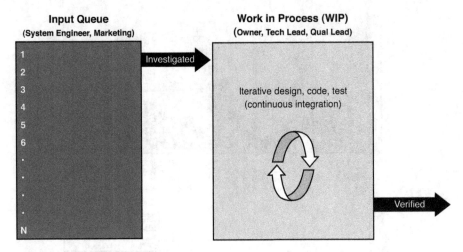

FIGURE 7.3   Managing Input Queue and Work in Process (WIP)

These roles are system engineer and marketing, which are discussed in detail in the section "Just-in-Time User Story Definition." In summary, the system engineer is in charge of translating the requirements into something meaningful that is well defined, with all collaborators identified. Each system engineer works very closely with marketing (and other feature requestors, such as customer assurance and manufacturing) to make sure that when a development team is ready for more work, it can pull a well-defined new requirement into WIP from the Input Queue and start working.

A prioritization scheme must not include only planned WIP (the next features on the 1-N list), but also any unplanned work (change requests or "bugs"). To avoid wreaking too much havoc on feature development, as change requests get submitted, we prioritize them based on whether someone is blocked by them (development or test) and by how critical they are from a customer perspective to fix (see Table 7.1). P1 change requests typically get fixed in anywhere from a day to a week because everyone drops what they're doing to work on them. The others take longer and that's okay; we've found a very good balance of feature focus versus change request responsiveness.

TABLE 7.1   Change Request Prioritization

Priority	Definition
P1	Drop everything and fix as soon as possible (critical customer escalation, or blocking internal development/test)
P2	Fix in the upcoming quarterly release (so it's okay to finish the feature you're currently working on before addressing these)
P3	Fix someday (don't put off any features in the current release to fix this)

If change requests are truly causing a large problem or are impacting the sprint objectives, we tag them as "[PUNCHLIST]" items. This gets immediate attention from multiple layers of management who work with Scrum-Masters to clear any impediment necessary, including moving resources around if needed to get them closed quickly.

In our process, fixes for change requests or bugs are integrated into the system in the same way as new features. They get integrated to main and get delivered to the field as part of standard quarterly releases. We keep the last quarterly release around for "hot fixes" for quick delivery to satisfy customer escalations when necessary, but only on an exception basis. We purposely focus nearly all our efforts on our upcoming release and delivering it on time with high quality.

This global prioritization/ranking of high-level sprint objectives, of features, and of change requests has truly freed us up to allow conflicts to be resolved at the right priority with just a few individuals, without a need for so many people to collaborate and meet. Scrums can be held at a small team level wherever needed, but nothing at a higher level. The priorities are even used by individual engineers in their day-to-day interactions. It's a very freeing concept.

We have found that the more we put the right simple rules of engagement in place, the fewer meetings we need to hold. So although there are individual feature teams in a given sprint that hold daily scrum meetings for status updates and removing impediments, we've found that having a larger "scrum of scrums" meeting daily or even three times per week just adds unneeded overhead—especially when we have 25 to 30 individual feature teams working on their collaborative efforts each sprint. We do have a once-a-week meeting with all the feature leads to address any major blocking issues (impediments) across the system and to make sure we're all on the same page with the sprint demos and overall sprint objectives, but the technical leads don't attend, and we don't talk about the individual features or "what did you just get done" and "what are you going to get done," as is typically discussed in a "scrum of scrums" meeting.

Just-in-Time User Story Definition

Don't think about early requirements/user story work as a planning activity. Treat it as what it really needs to be to streamline agile development and avoid all the estimating work that takes away from feature throughput: a prioritize and define process. Planning means "figure out how much work a feature is, do a work breakdown to the task level, and estimate when it will get done." We bypass this traditional "planning" completely in this model. One of the reasons for success is the close collaboration we've achieved by having all those involved in prioritizing and defining organized by the same end-to-end solution pillar areas. When new requests come in, the people in these roles efficiently accomplish both quick response and clean handoff, all working in prioritized, ranked order. To summarize, for each end-to-end pillar, we have a go-to person for each of the following roles; for each new feature request, people work closely and informally together to prioritize and define it (with the system engineer being the point person for shepherding it through the Input Queue until it's well defined):

- **System engineers**

  Their whole role is to work out the feature definition by taking new requested features from "new" to "investigated," where they are well defined and ready for handoff to the technical team.

- **Dedicated marketing leads**

  They prioritize feature requests as they come in so we always know what's most important. This is what Scrum calls the Product Owner.

- **Architect**

  Architects do early effort/risk assessment of features, and system engineers work closely with them to assure technology roadmaps are aligned with new requests.

- **Feature lead**

  Typically this person functions as a technical lead for the whole feature, reporting to the project manager who acts as the end-to-end lead among all collaborating teams.

Invest in System Engineering

If developers have coding or testing responsibilities, that's their focus. Until they are done with one feature, they really can't spend significant time driving the definition of a future feature. This means if they are the resource we're depending on for feature definition, we will never be able to evaluate incoming requests very quickly. Then requestors get disgruntled and either escalate or disengage, or we make the engineers' task switch so much that they are overwhelmed and less productive. Four years ago, we experimented with a role we call system engineer. We've gone from one or two in this role to now having eight full-time system engineers. They are experienced, well-respected engineers who have the talents to understand both the technology and the customer needs. They are also able to work closely across a very broad group of collaborators. They take requirements from an often nebulous request to something that is aligned with R&D roadmaps and capabilities. They consult with the technology architects and feature technical leads to assure that what is being considered is possible and best, but in an informal "part of every-day life" sort of way that doesn't take them away from development.

The system engineer's primary responsibility is to take ownership of feature definition from when a requirement is submitted until it's fully defined and all collaborating teams across the system are identified— what we call "Investigated." (See Figure 7.4 for the state model of require-ments.) The system engineers deliver a clean feature definition a month or two ahead of when a feature is targeted to be delivered. They then cleanly hand off responsibility of the requirement to an overall feature technical lead who drives it from "Investigated" to full delivery, including qualification in a feature kickoff meeting. This kickoff meeting includes the requester, all the collaborating engineers, test leads, and the feature technical leads. In this meeting, all the details of the feature as defined are reviewed, and everyone has a chance to ask clarifying questions before the development starts. Having the feature lead in place frees the system engineer to focus on the next requirement in the Input Queue. The system engineer defines the "what," the technical lead defines the "how," and the requirement owner (typically the project manager of the team most involved in delivering the feature) with the technical lead coordinates integration, delivery, and qualification. System engineers are a favorite of R&D because they help keep requests specific; they are a favorite of marketing because they help make sure the true feature intent is delivered; and they are a favorite of management because they enable productive delivery of features.

A huge side benefit we've found in this role is that the system engineers become such experts in their respective end-to-end feature pillar areas that they are very much in demand for consulting services on how should a feature work, which comes up regularly from developers and testers. Although we point them to the limited documentation we do provide, having a single point of contact within R&D for questions is a huge benefit. This role is critical to the success of an agile model where we minimize estimation and detailed early planning and instead focus on having just-in-time, clearly defined, end-to-end requirements ready in the system for teams to pull off the product backlog. These system engineers also become a help for our innovation pipeline as they see opportunities based on being close to customer requirements and the ability to deliver in R&D.

	Requirement Status	Responsible (to move to this state)	Description
System Engineer Drives	New	Author	Newly submitted (still part of unapproved backlog).
	Screened	System Engineer	Ready for Prioritization Team to review (description makes sense and is aligned with technology roadmaps).
	Proposed	Marketing (prioritization team)	**Prioritized/Ranked** for R&D (now on release backlog).
	Assigned	System Engineer	All collaborators identified and roles assigned (Owner, Tech Lead, Qual Lead).
	Investigated	System Engineer	Requirements **well-defined** and reviewed by all collaborators. Handoff to detailed design and coding/text activities. Two months prior to desired sprint for delivery.
Feature Owner Drives	Reviewed	Human Factors Engineer	Customer Experience design is complete (screen shots, strings). One month before desired Sprint for delivery
	Plan of Record	Owner (with Tech Lead/Qual Lead)	Code/test **design complete**. Sprint is assigned (not as a commitment, but as a best estimate of when will finish).
	Under Development	Owner	Have started writing code/tests.
	Implemented	Owner	Code all on main with unit test passing.
	Under Test	Owner	R&D system tests are on main and executing.
	Verified	Owner (with Qual Lead)	R&D system tests are all passing on Lead Product (or 90%+ passing with defects logged against every failure).

FIGURE 7.4   Requirements state model

The system engineer also assigns roles within the requirements database (HP Application Lifecycle Management (ALM) software, formerly QualityCenter) for all the key leads for each requirement (requestor, architect, owner, technical lead, and qualification lead), so it becomes easy to get reports out for each person as needed, and for everyone to know their collaborators. HP Application Lifecycle Management is an enterprise-level life cycle management tool we use for managing requirements, change requests, and test development and execution that we adopted after HP acquired Mercury Interactive in 2006.

To assure a proper feedback loop and keep the system engineers completely aware of any system constraints, after a feature is delivered they proactively engage again long enough to do a feature walkthrough. They set up a simple one-hour meeting with the requestor, the management chain responsible, and test partners, and walk through various user scenarios, trying out the feature and making sure it meets the original intent (obviously on some complex features, this gets more involved, but the same concepts apply).

It's been interesting to watch what happens when schedule pressures are high and someone invariably says, "We need to do away with the system engineer position," because they aren't delivering code or tests (the primary deliverables of a firmware or software organization). In a few cases, we've actually gone for a few months short-staffed for system engineers after someone gets promoted or pulled back to help deliver a feature. And without exception, the organization as a whole has come back and said, "Never mind—we absolutely need this role filled after all." It's definitely worth investing in!

Put Marketing in Charge of a Unified 1-N List

One of the breakthrough moments we had was when we were able to get the marketing department to go beyond slideware and engage in the details within the requirements area in Application Lifecycle Management. We created views of the data for them grouped by their area so they could go anytime and see what the priorities were, the current status, and any new items that had been requested that hadn't been prioritized. We have aligned system engineers and marketing along the same list of end-to-end feature pillar areas (such as security, device management, walkup use, printing, extensibility, and so on), where they can collaborate closely on user stories in each area.

One of our mantras with requirements is that "a requirement is the record of a conversation previously held." Having marketing aligned with system engineers makes this work well because a built-in relationship and verbal communication naturally happens instead of someone getting blindsided with new, urgent requests that just show up in a tool.

Involve the Technology Architects

The potential downside of not having the true technical experts in the organization proactively looking at new requests coming in is that some of the features may not fit with the current architecture or may be so much work within the architecture that it would be impossible to deliver them anytime soon. So once per quarter (plus real-time as needed), the system engineer sits down with the appropriate architect for each area and they briefly walk through the Input Queue and assign architectural risk and effort level (low/med/high/extreme) to each requirement. No work breakdown and no mapping to individual resources is done, so no real planning is done, either. What is created is familiarity with the list and any long-lead requirements are identified so we can get going on them earlier than later (Scrum recommends tackling the hardest problems first).

Use Project Managers as "Feature Leads"

All requirements start out as something we call "Product Requirements"—end-to-end capability for the customer/business, written as a user story. We have heavily utilized Mike Cohn's breakthrough book, *User Stories Applied: For Agile Software Development*. The system engineers break out each product requirement into multiple technical requirement children so that each team that needs to engage clearly has something to track and deliver. Project managers then not only have teams that report to them, but they also play the role of mini program managers. For the technical requirement children, this role is very straightforward and contained: deliver and qualify your part, attempting not to become a critical path for the overall product requirement or solution. For the parent product requirement, the owner must coordinate all delivery and qualification activities for that end-to-end feature. Sometimes this gets to be a very large multisprint effort. The manager shares this load with the technical lead, who fills the Scrum role of "product owner" for this feature. We've found that, though challenging, this has been a role critical to the success of the model, and the nice thing is that it also gives first-level project managers the higher visibility and experience that they often seek as they look for promotion opportunities. One related thing we've done is to put a test lead directly on each project team. There was a lot of discussion early on about having one test team where all test development and first-level triage would occur. This would have enabled us to be a bit more consistent in our test libraries and automation techniques, but having test developers sitting directly with feature developers and working for the feature leads has made quality much more infused into the organization.

Reuse Requirements and Test Tags for Scalability

You've heard of reusing software/firmware components. You've probably even heard of reusing tests. We do all that, but in addition we start upstream and make sure that the whole development and test process can be driven by requirements that can be reused. We are in a situation where the common HP FutureSmart Firmware must support many hardware products, from small printers to full-size large format copiers. Tests written for the large format copiers with extensive paper handling, multiple paper sizes, and a scanner don't make sense to run on a smaller product. Therefore, we needed an efficient process for making sure which of our approximately 30,000 automated tests should run on which product. After a new requirement is delivered (on what we call the lead product), we have to make sure it's also tested on every other product that applies. So at the time we define each requirement, we select each product (or product line) that it applies to (called "applicable products"). This information is then used to feed test selection tools so after the feature is verified on the lead product, it can automatically be selected to be executed on each other applicable product. This early, simple, requirements-based productization is critical to scaling large-scale agile to multiple products that must have each feature tested. Otherwise, it's a very hands-on, manual test-focused approach, especially when future features need to work on already released products (which is a fundamental objective of HP FutureSmart Firmware).

This all sounds great, and it works very streamlined now, especially after we put a tool in place to autocreate test lists per product based on the applicable products data. But we didn't start out this way. All of our focus was on creating reusable firmware. After the first two years of this initiative, and we had our first few new products out the door, we started getting ready for the next products and realized we basically had to start over with our test planning. We did a copy/paste of the tests from the most similar product, and then started evaluating everything to see what still applied and what was missing. This was a very manual, time-intensive process. Even when we completed it for the next products, all of a sudden we looked up and realized we'd delivered new features and had to go back to close those new test holes for all the products. Like almost all good ideas, it takes a painful process to drive us to change to a simple but powerful solution, such as reuse requirements, especially for test selection.

For our example, this meant thinking through how we would want to organize our automated tests for metrics and execution. We grouped requirements and tests to make it easy to select which tests to run on which products. This realization came to us after we had a large number of automated tests in place, which meant that fixing it required a big effort with a lot of rework. It is really a key learning from our school of hard knocks, which we hope we can help you avoid. Before you start writing a large number of automated tests, spend some time thinking through your business and how this should be organized. Are there different tests that would make sense to run at certain times? Are there different ways you might want to report subsets of the test reports? If you can think through these ideas before you start writing tests, and develop a standard for tagging the requirements or tests before getting started, it will potentially save you a lot of pain and rework later.

Commit by Delivering, Not by Estimating

As new requirements and change requests are submitted, there's a real push—especially if the requests are coming directly from the sales organization to enable big deals—to have development teams go into "estimation mode" and figure out when we can commit to having a new feature or change request finished and delivered. *We strive to avoid this like the plague.* If a new feature comes in, we make sure it's aligned with our strategy and then prioritize it on the 1-N list where the business wants it in relation to the current feature backlog. If it's a critical customer commitment, it typically goes right to the top of the list, a system engineer starts defining it immediately, and it typically gets delivered in the next quarterly release (or the one following, depending on where we are in the cycle).

For change requests, we don't do planning or estimating at all. We just make it a priority 1 if needed, which means we drop everything and fix it. We did staff a dedicated team for change requests submitted from the field so we can get quick traction on all of them, regardless of the priority. Typically, we need to answer a customer within a week or two as to whether and when we will address the issue they've found. Historically, this meant doing a cost/benefit justification, including an estimation effort to scope what it would take. But now with a single firmware code base supporting several product lines, we don't bother with any of this. Thanks to our previously discussed automated/streamlined integration and testing processes, we frequently get a change request fixed and fully tested within a day, and most are fixed within a week after we start in on them.

In Scrum, burndown charts are considered a critical and daily part of the process where engineers provide up-front task estimates and then give daily updates to those estimates throughout each four-week sprint. The primary value of the burndown chart is to predict when all the work will be completed. It is a way to show "work remaining versus time" and "are we on track." Although they probably work great for some businesses, we found two problems with burndown charts for us. First, the time spent doing daily updates to each task estimate was time that could have been spent accomplishing more tasks instead of estimating what was remaining. Second, by its very nature, the goal of the burndown chart is to get to zero. That means we're optimizing for predictability, not throughput.

Where's the incentive to set stretch goals? Or the incentive to try to complete a feature that may not be high-confidence for the sprint but a huge benefit to the business or customer? A few teams used them for their own work, but we never adopted them globally.

Although it's important not to constantly overdrive the system in agile—to push too hard and thus cause burn-out—it is still important to have a sense of passion and excitement about what can be accomplished. We found that burndown charts and the process around them tended to take away from the passion and made things too methodical and focused on the estimating versus the delivery. We have alternative methods for tracking sprint progress by continuously tracking the status of requirements, change requests, and testing. And many teams do daily standups. But none of this involves the daily reestimating, or anything that takes away from feature throughput. We also have other ways to keep from taking on too much work and help keep things at a maintainable pace. We use sprint objectives and the sprint kickoff to look at the number of user stories at a global level to make sure we're in line with our historical capacity (described earlier in this chapter). Each team also looks at its sprint-to-sprint history of how many requirements (user stories) they've delivered and makes sure the coming sprint is of similar size for them. This works well to keep Work in Process (WIP) down but without the overhead of burndown charts. We also differentiate between the critical requirements for the sprint versus the bonus ones, so there are always features that are just fine to slip out a sprint when there's new discovery or we run into trouble.

We found another way to build excitement and focus: Before the sprint starts, we pick demos for the sprint checkpoint we do right after a sprint finishes. It's been amazing what a team can accomplish when it knows it has the opportunity to shine during a demo in front of management. (As Scrum states, our goal with sprint checkpoints is to do a lot more demos than slides.) One of the ways we've kept focus on continuous integration and quality is to ask two questions after every demo: "Is the code all integrated?" followed by "Do you have an automated test?"

Convincing the Business: Agile Planning Is Okay

As you can imagine, when we first told marketing and the product program managers that we were no longer going to give them a commitment to the full feature list one year before product introduction, they didn't like it one bit. So we scurried around a bit to figure out the WIIFM (What's in It for Me) for them so they would go along. We were unwilling to continue down our prior path anymore because it was wasting so many resources that could have been delivering products and features. Here are the benefits of agile planning that we used to help convince our marketing and product program partners that it was okay to change:

- *Firmware will still commit to basic new product support one year in advance.*

  This meant prioritizing product turn-on and delivery/ qualification ahead of new features, and learning to separate out new feature requests from "make my product work." Key to this was getting a solutions marketing group set up who treated new features/solutions as their own roadmap, completely independent of the delivery product hardware platform. Although it initially took some convincing that the product teams could survive without being in control of every feature they would get, this worked well for most features where the product teams were not the real experts anyway, such as security, digital sending, extensibility and third-party solutions, fleet management, and other high-end features.

- *You will get 20% more features this way.*

  This was a leap of faith for people because seeing is believing, but we explained that we were spending 20% of our engineering resources doing all this detailed planning to do early commitments. And most of that planning ended up being a complete waste because everything had changed when, six months later, we got back to reengaging on the details of each feature we previously "committed."

- *You get to decide what we work on first.*

  We established a 1-N feature request list, and the combined marketing teams got to decide the order. In a lot of ways, this helped them feel much more in control than before. It was critical to have a single point of contact in marketing across all features to help prioritize new features. Otherwise, we got a lot of behaviors where the squeaky wheel gets the grease (whoever is loudest or most emotional about their request became first in queue). In addition to a single point of contact in marketing, for tactically putting together a 1-N list, it also required a governance model where the different business leaders came together regularly to review/approve the 1-N request list.

- *We'll actually listen to your last-minute requests.*

  Every time a competitor comes up with a cool new feature we don't have or a large sales opportunity comes up that is dependent on a new solution we don't yet have in place, put it at the top of the list, ahead of all the other Input Queue features that we haven't started, and instead of having to wait 12-18 months, we can deliver it with much faster turnaround. This was the clincher. Although the product teams and product marketing still had their doubts, this convinced them to be willing to take the plunge into this wacky new world of agile. This happened recently with the new "HP ePrint" initiative. This would historically have taken a few years to get into the system, but with this model, we were able to do it in a matter of months. We recently had a medium-size feature into the system and verified within a month of when the request came in.

We also had some conditions we set to make this work for the development organization:

- *We commit by delivering, not by planning.*

  With a few exceptions (with high-profile field escalations/customer commitments), we no longer take away engineering resources to plan. In most cases, a feature transitions directly from Input Queue to Work in Process to Verified using just-in-time planning. We still get pockets of people wanting us to "commit now," but we've held fast to this principle.

- *We reserve the right to continue working on features right up to the last minute in a release without precommitting to them.*

  This sometimes means that marketing can't message a feature they want, but we all decided that it's better to get a feature and not have time to message it than to commit to a risky feature, message it, and then end up slipping schedule. Delivering on a consistent rhythm is more important than any one feature. Marketing quickly learned that if they wanted to message something badly enough, they would put it near the top of the list.

Summary

Planning has its place, but it needs to be a limited place. It's critical to do architectural and roadmap planning to assure we are set up for whatever large, new market or business needs are coming along next. But this is not the scheduling/estimating planning that we formerly spent so much time doing. So although the business will naturally attempt to get us to commit early and often and with great detail, we've decided planning needs to stay in that limited place and not take over development activities and lower our throughput.

Do you really need the predictability you've always had? Or have you really had the predictability you thought you did? Or are you wasting precious resources to do those planning activities that lower feature throughput and give false hope or dangerous commitments that drive the development organization and the business crazy?

With the right model and "predict through trends" tools, and the right investment in key roles in marketing and system engineering, it's possible to not only avoid slowdowns to feature development, but to also give the business a realistic sense of what to expect and have a strong working relationship with all parts of the business. Focusing on roadmaps, prioritization, and then clean just-in-time feature definition instead of on scheduling/estimating activities has been a refreshing approach that keeps us focused on optimizing feature throughput instead of predictability.

We're finding that having predictable, on-time regular releases so new products can always launch on time is more important than knowing exactly what features will land in which release. Doing sufficient planning for the basic schedule and a few business-critical features that can't afford to slip is the right thing to do and is the right level to focus on. Never say never, but in three years of large-scale agile, we haven't yet met a feature that we couldn't deliver in a reasonable time with this model.

This is one area where a lot of our processes are similar to the leading edge ideas in the agile community, but the terminology is different. Before you go down the path of fundamentally changing your planning processes, we highly recommend that your thought leaders in this area take the time to read *Agile Software Requirements* by Dean Leffingwell. It is an excellent reference with great ideas that could have saved us a lot of time. Dean provides details that are very valuable about how to make this work in a large organization.

There are many similarities to what we did, and his book also provides some great ideas that we missed by not leveraging the agile community. We ended up taking different approaches in some areas, the most significant of these areas being the act of planning. Instead of the teams coming together once per release to have a detailed, all-hands-on-deck planning meeting, in our approach this is an ongoing process where user stories are constantly working through the definition, scope, and priority process. The project managers then work with their individual teams to determine when they can make solid commitments in the current sprint and rough estimates for the next two sprints. If these commit dates are unacceptable, then the project manager starts working with marketing and the program managers to agree on trade-offs and options. This tends to happen offline on a regular basis instead of in a major meeting per sprint. There are probably different advantages to each approach.

Chapter 8

UNIQUE CHALLENGES OF
ESTIMATING LARGE INNOVATIONS

The previous chapter provided an overview of how we estimate schedules and feature delivery in an agile environment when the system engineers can do a good job estimating the work for each team or, even better, if the requirements are broken down into two to four weeks' worth of work for an engineer. We've found this works great for 80 to 90% of the features being asked for. But some features or innovations have large architectural dependencies and are much harder to predict. These initiatives typically involve a lot of discovery and prototyping, and even doing significant investigations into multiple alternatives. The biggest example is a large re-architecture effort like ours. How do you proceed with planning and estimation for these situations involving so much uncertainty? This chapter provides insight into the unique challenges faced when trying to plan this type of effort.

We start the chapter with an overview of the waterfall approach compared with the agile approach; then we describe the specific challenges of using agile for large innovations and getting the business to go along with this approach.

Waterfall Approach and Challenges

Before describing how we approach these types of challenges, it is probably best to start by explaining more about the waterfall method and why the agile thought leaders headed down a different path. The waterfall method starts by documenting all the requirements and architecture plans. This is followed by an extensive scheduling step where all the work is planned, including dependencies among the different components. The organization then starts executing these plans with an extensive development phase. The final step is to integrate all the components and complete the final qualification process.

The idea of the waterfall approach is to do enough up-front work to fully understand the program so you can successfully commit to scope, resources, and schedule. This waterfall approach and the history of different agile techniques is covered well by Dean Leffingwell in *Scaling Software Agility: Best Practices for Large Enterprises*. He points out that the move to more agile approaches occurred because the waterfall approach was not working very well. There was discovery during development that tended to push schedules. Additionally the integration and qualification step resulted in long ugly endgames that frequently also pushed schedules (see Figure 8.1). The idea of doing the work up-front to fix scope, resources, and schedule was great in concept, but for large SW projects, agile approaches were developed to address the reality that waterfall projects had a poor track record of success.

Agile Approach

The agile community set out to find a different approach for development to address the shortcomings of the waterfall method. There are several changes in the development process targeted at the long, ugly integration and qualification cycles:

- **Continuous Integration**

  Starting integration from the beginning to catch integration issues and uncertainty early before writing lots of code that heads down the wrong path.

- **Test Automation**

  Ensuring the quality of code and keeping the product stable as new capabilities are developed. This is designed to make the qualification part of the ongoing process instead of a separate event at the end.

- **Development Sprints** (or MMs in our case)

  The intent here is to develop innovation using a fixed rhythm with a smaller set of capabilities being completely developed through integration and qualification on a fixed cycle.

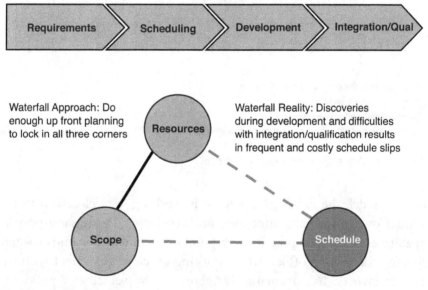

FIGURE 8.1   Classic SW/FW waterfall development model

The objective of these changes is to have a constantly evolving and improving code base that can be released to customers on a regular frequency. The waterfall cycle is broken down into smaller sprints where a subset of capabilities is completely developed and added to the existing code base every two to four weeks (see Figure 8.2). These adjustments enable changing how you manage the program resources, scope, and schedule triangle. It recognizes that resources are the least flexible leg of the triangle because these are human programmers, and it takes a significant amount of time to find programmers and get them up to speed on a new code base. The schedule leg of the triangle is fixed by design in agile by driving to a regular delivery rhythm. In the agile approach, the scope is the leg used to absorb the program uncertainty.

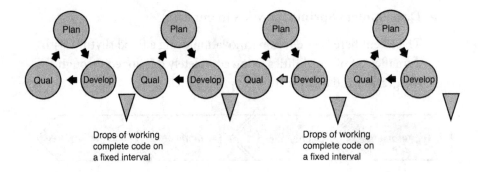

Drops of working complete code on a fixed interval

Drops of working complete code on a fixed interval

- Fully qualified code drops on a fixed schedule
- Frequent small integrations
- Short planning and delivery cycles
- Working a well-prioritized product backlog (requirements, solutions, etc.)

FIGURE 8.2   Agile development paradigm

In this model, the development team is working very closely with the product owner to make sure they are developing the highest-priority capabilities first. Agile practitioners point out numerous examples where allowing the scope to float, while working on close alignment with the product owners, has dramatically increased the velocity of providing value to the customers. In the waterfall method, all the must-have features would have to be developed before going through an endgame to deliver anything to the customer. In agile, working code is available on a regular frequency, with the highest-priority features coming in first. In this model, the development team can interact with the product owner or, in the ideal case, the customer, to determine when enough functionality is available to start deploying. Using this model, agile practitioners have numerous examples where after delivering less than 50% of the original must-have features, the customer is happy with the product and is no longer requesting more. In the waterfall approach, it would have taken much longer to deliver any value because there are no regular drops, and the final qualification and integration would never have started until all the original must-have features were delivered.

This approach dramatically improves the time to value for customers, because they don't have to wait a long time before deploying, and they are getting the highest value first. Instead of having to wait for a big bang, they get smaller installments on a regular basis, and after working with the code, they have a much better understanding of what really matters versus what felt like a good idea in the beginning. One of the big advantages of agile is that you can respond to changes to what is needed based on what customers learn from using the product, and delivery of the value is not pushed out by lower-priority capabilities. All this is enabled by a well-prioritized but evolving list of priorities developed by the product owner and a development process that delivers a steady stream of fully qualified new capabilities on a stable code base. How we created these capabilities for the HP LaserJet Printer business is documented in the previous chapters.

Challenging Situations with the Agile Approach: Large Architectural Efforts

After you have these processes and capabilities in place, the planning process works fairly smoothly, except when you have big architectural changes or development that is completely new, with large degrees of uncertainty. In these instances, it is hard to estimate the work; and in a lot of cases, the scope is not as flexible as the ideal agile scenario described previously. In these cases, what do you do? How do you let the business know what to expect? How do you plan the work and get going?

At this point, it is probably helpful to share a story from early in the director's career, when he was a section manager working in a waterfall delivery process. Here's the story in his own words:

> One day the program manager came to me requesting my help. We had been doing the detailed planning process for the next 12-month delivery cycle. The help the program manager needed was that one of the project managers had a plan that showed the must-have capabilities coming in 6 months late. We could not afford to slip the programs, so he needed me to sit down with the team and work through all the details in the plan to make sure we met the required schedule. The project manager and her technical lead came to the meeting fully prepared with stacks of paper showing why the schedule was going to take 6 months longer than was required. At this point I grabbed all the paper, folded it up, and put it away in my desk. Next, I looked at the technical lead and said, "I want you to get some working code up and going as quickly as possible. I want you to hack and slash where you have to but I want working code by the end of the month. Then at that point, after you have been working in the code and understanding the major obstacles, I am willing to start talking about the schedule again." The technical lead went heads down writing code for a month, and every time he found a point where he needed to make a hack to get the prototype working, he documented the real work on a whiteboard outside his cube. At the end of the month, he came back with a clear list of all the work and a plan showing why they would be done 4 months before the program needed the code.

The reason we point out this story is that frequently, to understand what it takes to deliver something new with a high degree of uncertainty, you need to get in and start writing code (in other words, "prototype to remove uncertainty"). The most important step is for the engineers to start learning and figuring out what needs to be done before you can start planning or scheduling. In Chapter 1, we talked about bringing up a new architecture with thin slices and prototypes. It is our belief that this is the first step in any large architectural effort or work with large amounts of discovery. You should start with the biggest technical challenges, the largest areas of uncertainty, or the most foundational parts of the architecture (see Figure 8.3). This effort should also be led out by the most experienced developers because the patterns developed and the architectural approach defined here will lay the foundation for all the additional work.

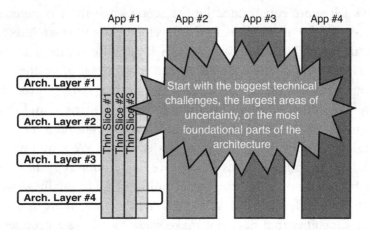

FIGURE 8.3   Thin-slice approach to bringing up a new architecture

During this phase, you should also expect to throw away as much or more code as you keep. The key point is to learn as much as you can as fast as you can and make sure you are developing a solid foundation for your architecture.

Only after you have sufficiently developed some thin slices and the basic layers of the architecture do you have a good foundation for estimating the schedule for the additional work. In this example, after developing the first thin slice for application #1, you have probably learned enough to provide good schedule estimates for building out all the slices for application #1, including constraints and error coding instead of just the happy path. You probably have a better idea of what the schedule will be for application #2 but not a great idea until you develop the first thin slice in application #2. This process can then continue as you start building out the other applications. In the agile approach, the idea is that you start with the highest-priority applications first so that you could potentially start delivering value to the customers before all the applications are complete. Only then do you have enough information to start putting together a meaningful schedule with planned customer drops.

This approach describes the theory and a feasible approach. In our experience, the practical application has been a little more difficult because we have felt more constrained by the scope knob than is espoused in the agile model. For example, in the development and re-architecture of HP FutureSmart Firmware, we had very limited flexibility in scope. We were bringing out a new code base to an existing set of customers who were expecting it to match the capabilities of their current products. So although we did continuous integration, test automation, and development sprints, we weren't able to manage our scope knob, and the program uncertainty was absorbed in the delivery schedule. We were implementing a lot of the agile practices to improve our productivity, but we were unable to leverage one of the biggest advantages. Additionally, as we work through other efforts to bring up new architecture, there is a certain baseline capability that does not make sense to release a product without. Therefore, while agile has the right approach of driving to a regular rhythm with always releasable code, there are times when scope is not as flexible as we would like. The agile approach for these types of challenges is to have the product owner work closely with the development team, constantly track progress each sprint, and make real-time decisions around when to release for deployment.

Change Management and Integrating with the Business

There's another big challenge we have found (and are still working through) that is unique to large-scale agile. In small-scale agile, there is a real focus on the close linkages of a product owner working with the team to drive the release schedule. How do we scale these linkages in a large enterprise where multiple layers of management and different organizations are dependent on the deliverables? Especially in an environment where the expectation is to use a traditional waterfall approach of committing to a schedule (with all the details) and then making it happen. How does the executive driving the business ensure the organization is aligning with strategic directions and aggressively driving the organization with this level of uncertainty? How does the development organization interact with the broader business to ensure it is not overcommitted to impossible schedules before the appropriate discovery is complete? How does the development organization ensure that not too much work is being driven into the organization so that nothing can be completed? Remember, as we pointed out earlier in the lean principles, **the more you try to do, the less that actually gets done**. There also needs to be a manageable amount of work in the system so tasks can be completed and the organization can feel successful about its deliverables.

We have found this transition and interaction on new architectural work to be a big challenge and frustration for both the business and the development team. The development team feels like it is working on all the right things and bringing up the thin slices as quickly as possible. They are describing what they are learning and the progress on architectural approaches. At the same time, the business side just wants to hear that the team is committed to the schedule and has a detailed plan to deliver. The idea that all the development team wants to talk about is what they are learning can be very frustrating for business leaders. The interaction results in a team that feels overcommitted before they understand the real work and a business organization that feels a need to drive harder for commitments because the development teams obviously don't understand the importance or the priorities.

Breaking this logjam will probably require educating the business side on agile methodologies and approaches. It will also require the development teams to ensure they are addressing the business expectations and that they can show they are aligned on the priorities and aggressively driving the objectives. The development teams will also need to make sure they can describe when they will understand enough about the work so they can commit to delivering the minimal viable product or solution. The basic concepts of interacting with the product owner to track progress and making the decisions around timing for the first deployable drop apply, but it is difficult to scale this approach to a large organization with busy executives. On a smaller scale, the product owner is a person who is interacting with the team on a regular basis. On a larger scale, the business side has the same needs, but it is difficult to create the same level of intimacy with the development team making real-time trade-offs and priorities.

The solution we are still working to develop will probably require some alignment on expectations for tracking progress on the thin-slice development. The business side needs to see the commitment to the task and the progress by the team. The development team will also need to help the business side understand when they think they will have learned enough to commit to a schedule for the minimal viable product. The development team should additionally help the management team understand what can be delivered when, so managers feel they have some influence over the minimal viable product definition. The two groups will also need to agree on a process or approach for committing to schedule and scope on these types of efforts.

Summary

As you can see, there are some significant challenges with planning and schedule commitments for new architectural investments or large innovations. We are still learning and evolving in terms of how we scale the approaches of the product owner to interfacing with a large enterprise with several constituencies. The idea of writing some code, setting a solid foundation, and creating some thin slices is important before committing to a schedule. At the same time, the development team needs to ensure they are developing an effective approach for interacting with the broader organization.

Chapter 9

OUR TAKE ON PROJECT MANAGEMENT FOR LARGE-SCALE AGILE

When we started working with Jim Highsmith on the first early reviews of this manuscript, we had already included the chapters on our general management approach (Chapter 5, "The Real Secret to Success in Large-Scale Agile"), how we changed our build, integration, and test processes (Chapter 6, "Continuous Integration and Quality Systems"), and our short and long-range planning (Chapter 7, "Taming the Planning Beast"). We thought that described what we do quite well, but Jim kept pushing, asking us, "How do you really do project management? What are the roles and responsibilities? Who does what and how do you keep all these people organized and delivering?" In a large agile organization, it is hard to make it clear exactly how everything works because it is constantly changing and evolving, but we will try to explain it here.

At the top R&D level, we have three different types of roles that we use to help drive this large organization. First are the program managers who are responsible for leading deliveries across the organization and interfacing with our partners. Second are the section managers who own the resources in the organization and are accountable for the deliverables (and the project managers who report to them and who directly manage all the engineers, their deliverables to successful completion, and the

101

quality of the solutions and products). Third are the architects that help make sure we are driving the right technical priorities and helping to lead us through tough technical challenges, including scalability and performance of the solution.

Oversight and Priority: Program Managers

To better understand how it all works, it is probably best to start with the program manager view. We have three separate program manager roles in the lab, each managing a different phase of the life cycle. The first is for product turn on and interacting with all the product teams. As we stated in the planning chapter, we have completely separated what it takes to run a new product from what new features are important to add to differentiate our fleet from competitive products. This program manager is fully dedicated to working with the different product teams to understand and negotiate what system capabilities they need, and when, to keep the product development on track. He ensures all the requirements for product turn on are documented and prioritized in Application Life-cycle Management (ALM) software (formerly Quality Center) so we can track and manage them. This program manager also works with the different product hardware teams to understand the stability of the code on their products and also prioritizes change requests needed to keep their programs on track.

The second program manager is responsible for coordinating the delivery of the code as we drive to create new functionality and a release to the field (that we call bit release). This program manager oversees requirements prioritized for each release, test passing rates, and the prioritizing of change requests to keep the overall release on track. He also works closely with other R&D teams and the final QA teams to coordinate our deliverables with those groups. A big focus is also improving efficiency/ effectiveness in our development processes and quality.

The third program manager works with the organizations requesting new features to make sure they are defined and prioritized correctly and well represented in Application Lifecycle Management. He and his team of system engineers work to stay ahead of development by feeding a consistent stream of new work in prioritized order to all the teams. They constantly work through trade-off discussions each release as they manage the sprint backlog and product/release backlog of requirements.

All three of these program managers strive to clarify, prioritize, and make sure we capture all the work across the system to ensure the deliverables are coming together. They are all also responsible for understanding what is working and where the organization is struggling. Most all of this is managed as they work together to come up with the sprint objectives each month, and then monitor and manage to help achieve them.

Accountability: Section Managers

The section managers are second-level people managers in the organization (managing 5 to 6 teams totaling 40 to 50 people) and also have budget responsibility. They report directly to the director of engineering and are responsible for making sure that we have clarity around the priorities from the three program managers and for ensuring the teams hit their deliverables. As you can imagine, with three program managers trying to drive work into the system, it is easy to get overcommitted with conflicting priorities. The job of the section managers is to integrate all the requests and make sure we have clear priorities for the project managers and their teams; they make sure we have realistic commitments across the system as we look at the requirements coming from product turn on, new feature innovations, and internal productivity/re-architecture/testability initiatives. Their job is also to understand where the teams are struggling and to work with them to find creative solutions to meet the objectives or work with their peers to get help. The section managers provide resource sharing across the organization to help manage the bottlenecks.

They are not embedded directly into the agile process, but are there to tackle the difficult issues where additional people or money may be needed to help solve problems.

Although the project managers are not at the lab level (they all report directly to the section managers), we need to call them out very explicitly here. They are the ones in the trenches making things happen. We expect project managers to wear two hats: they are people managers of their direct team, but they are also requirement owners for driving end-to-end solutions to fully validated completion. Often, these solutions are complex, and they become the "virtual feature team" managers across the organization. They, along with their technical lead and qualification lead for that feature, must make sure it all comes together. This is where the day-to-day agile process really is driven. Daily scrums are typically driven by the feature technical lead and/or the project manager as they manage a virtual feature team across as many teams in the organization as needed.

Robustness and Scalability: Architects

The architects' job is to look across the technology to make sure we are driving the right investments in our processes to improve productivity and the code, to ensure we are prioritizing fixing weaknesses in our architecture. Even after completing a whole new architecture, we've found that it must be a living, breathing, continuously evolving framework in order to keep the business moving forward. They also lead SWAT efforts around key attributes of the system (memory, performance, reliability, security, and so on) that tend to suffer over time if not monitored regularly and architected.

Putting It All Together

This description of roles is an oversimplification, but it provides a good overview, including how work gets into the system and gets done. The interesting part, though, is how this all gets integrated at the staff level in terms of priorities and plans. The setting of MM (Mini Milestone or sprint) priorities and objectives and tracking the deliverables is where the rubber really meets the road. The priorities and objectives are where we start hashing out all the requests from the different program managers, and the section managers work toward realistic plans their teams can deliver. We have found that doing a good job here can take discussion across two weeks for a large organization, so we have learned to start during the last week of each MM when we have a better understanding of what will get done during the previous MM. This discussion of new objectives usually starts at the overall R&D staff level and then needs to go through a few iterations at the program managers' forum (a team of all the project managers led by the program managers), project team meetings, and the section manager's staff meetings before we align on the objectives. This process draws passion out of everyone involved and tends to be contentious because everyone has a great list of ideas it would be nice to achieve in each MM that quickly overcome our capacity if left unchecked. You can tell when we are getting close to the right set of objectives when you get a reaction from a section manager like, "I can't do everything on the list because I need to get through these things in this priority order if I am going to be successful in the long term." At that point, you start writing down the priorities and documenting the objectives for that MM. This monthly process does just what is needed to manage our Work in Process (WIP) effectively to avoid overwhelming the organization.

After that, the job is to track those deliverables and understand what is working versus what needs to be improved during the next MM. We continue this process MM after MM until we look back and realize we have made significant progress with our development processes and are starting to transform our business. It is not always clean and is probably not a clear case study in program management, but it has enabled us to dramatically improve our productivity and business results.

Summary

In striving to make large-scale agile work, it is critical to figure out who the decision makers and communicators are, to establish clear roles for each, and then work to get focus on how they can most effectively lead the organization to greatness in an iterative way. The engagement that comes from using these organizational leaders to align and drive on monthly sprint objectives produces a close-knit, effective large-scale organization that can drive forward on the right business objectives with complete focus and clarity of priority.

Chapter 10

ORGANIZATIONAL APPROACH: MANAGING TO DISADVANTAGES

The pure academic approach to agile practice has some very specific approaches to organization. We've leveraged some of these but have chosen not to follow others as we've scaled agile to our large organization. This is important to point out because, like architecture, organization provides a lot of leverage for driving changes in behavior and results. However, there are advantages and disadvantages to different organizational approaches. The classical example of the impact of organizational approaches is provided by studying the history of about 80 years of R&D at DuPont.[1] In their history, they ended up switching from centralized corporate R&D labs to distributed divisional R&D roughly every decade—in the process, losing about one year of productivity making each transition (see Table 10.1). The reason they were driven to change is that although each approach has advantages, each also has disadvantages. DuPont would grow so frustrated with the disadvantages of their most current approach that over time (about once a decade), they would decide they needed to drive a major organizational change to get the advantage of the other approach.

---

1. Based on David Hounshell and John Smith Jr. *Science and Corporate Strategy: Du Pont R&D 1902-1980*, New York: Cambridge University Press, 1988.

TABLE 10.1   Overall R&D Organization Options

Centralized Corporate R&D	Divisional R&D
Advantages: ■ Long-range strategic investment ■ More efficient use of resources	Advantages: ■ Meeting market needs ■ Commercializing innovations
Disadvantages: ■ Limited ties to the businesses ■ Disconnect from the customer	Disadvantages: ■ All incremental improvements and no significant breakthroughs

The thing DuPont didn't keep in mind with these organizational approaches is that after you have chosen an approach, you don't need to worry about getting the advantages of that design because it will come naturally. Where you need to provide management focus is on addressing the disadvantages of your organizational choice. This was true for R&D at DuPont, and it is true for large-scale agile organizational decisions in general.

In this chapter, we present three examples of our choices for organizational approach for large-scale agile. The three areas are test ownership organization, component versus feature-based organization, and traditional versus self-managed teams. In some areas we decided to organize as recommended by the agile community, but in others we decided to go against the standard agile approach. In each area we highlight the advantages and disadvantages of each approach, including why we chose the approach we did, and how we are achieving the natural advantages of our choices while attempting to proactively manage key aspects to minimize the disadvantages of our choices.

Test Ownership Organization

The first organizational approach we will address is having a centralized test organization versus distributing the test resources on each team. The advantages and disadvantages of each are listed in Table 10.2.

TABLE 10.2 Test Organization Options

Distributed Test Resources	Centralized Test Organization
Advantages: ■ The development team owns the quality of its code. ■ Investments in development and test will be balanced because the team is not done until it is developed and tested.	Advantages: ■ Independent validation of quality. ■ Focused investment on improving testing processes and tools. ■ Coordinated test plans and test coverage.
Disadvantages: ■ No separate group validating quality. ■ No ownership for driving improvements in test processes and tools. ■ No ownership for driving a coordinated approach to validating quality across all the groups.	Disadvantages: ■ Feature development and code writing tends to exceed the capacity of the test organization's ability to keep up. ■ Development teams don't completely own the quality of their code.

When we started this journey, there was a big debate in the management team over the best approach. We started with a mixture of distributed in most sections but centralized in one section. In the beginning, the test architect got all the different test leads together to understand how everyone was testing before we started on the new architectural investment. What we found was that every test lead or test developer had created a harness or test framework for testing his or her part of the code. The review showed a lot of commonality but a lack of leverage across the groups. Because we were driving for productivity improvements, we decided to go for a common approach all the testers could leverage. Thus was born our Common Test Framework, or CTF (described in Chapter 12, "The Right Tools: Quantum Leaps in Productivity").

At this time, we could have decided to go with a centralized test organization to avoid disadvantages we had with things like independent test harnesses. This was debated extensively in the management team, and in the end we developed a hybrid model that feels like a good balance. The test leads and test developers are all distributed across the development teams that are responsible for owning the quality of their code. In addition, we have in place a centralized team that owns driving CTF, automation infrastructure, test processes, and approaches (remember, this is a large organization).

This all describes our internal-to-R&D testing (both unit/component level and firmware subsystem level) and is focused primarily on fully automated testing using harnesses and simulators/emulators (also described in more detail in Chapter 12). We also partner with an independent Quality Assurance (QA) group within our HP division; they test the overall system at the product level on final hardware in complex environments with all other parts of the solution to ensure the entire system is working well together and will be a high quality experience in the customer environment. Anything they find is considered a test escape from the development teams that own the quality of their code.

The net result of our organizational approach is interesting to observe in the conversations and changes we are seeing. After going down this path for a while and expecting our development teams to start owning their quality, we had teams coming back wanting to change our plans for testing. When we started, the testers wrote all their code in Visual Basic and the developers used C#. Teams started saying this didn't make any sense because it was hard for them to switch back and forth between development and test. Additionally, Visual Basic was not a very powerful tool, even though it was all most of the test developers knew. Therefore, the teams that were leading the effort to start owning their code were the ones that started transitioning their tests to a common programming language. At this point, we knew we were starting to get the desired advantages of having test ownership distributed to each team.

Another telling discussion was when a project manager came up to the director and said he felt that we should switch back to centralized test development because his test development was not keeping up and he had to keep pulling developers off of writing code to help with test development. The director laughed a bit and pointed out to him that is exactly the behavior we want. So although he appreciated his idea for improvement, we are going to keep things the way they are for that very reason.

The advantage we get from having a centralized team for CTF and the testing processes is that we have a team that is constantly reminding us if we are not making the progress on testing infrastructure required for our organization to be successful. This team is also constantly pushing on improving the test speed of CTF so we can maximize the effectiveness of our 10,000 hours of testing each day. If one thing has been consistent through our transformation, it is that we have underestimated the importance and investment in our test processes. If everything test related was distributed in an organization this large, we wouldn't have sufficient visibility to the problem or the drive to make the required improvements. Although our organization of test isn't perfect, we believe the current approach is giving us a nice balance of getting the developers to own the quality of their code while driving the efficiencies in test required for a large-scale agile implementation.

Component versus Feature Organization

From a pure agile perspective, the general community recommends organizing by feature teams that can completely own the features—from definition through delivery and qualification. Table 10.3 presents the general advantages and disadvantages of traditional component team R&D organization versus feature teams.

TABLE 10.3   Developer Organization Options

Component Teams	Feature Teams
Advantages:	Advantages:
■ The team owns the code and has a deep level understanding of its specific component.	■ Complete ownership and clear accountability for driving successful completion of new capabilities.
■ The team owns the unit and subsystem test coverage of its component.	■ Focus on business value.
■ The team owns the performance and stability of its component	■ Ability to move resources and do whatever it takes to complete the new capability.

Disadvantages:	Disadvantages:
▪ The inability to drive a feature to completion because different teams are working to different priorities. ▪ Lack of complete ownership for delivering a new feature to completion.	▪ Lack of clear ownership for prioritizing technical debt. ▪ Lack of clear ownership for architecture integrity. ▪ Resource planning for technical expertise.

In our case, we chose to stay organized by component teams, as is the case with some other large-scale agile implementations. This decision was driven a lot by the fact that we were bringing up a new architecture rather than adding features to an existing, stable code base. As you can see in the table, this organization choice means we have components that are well maintained for the future, continuously evolving for scalability, and highly qualified. But getting end-to-end features managed and delivered can be challenging because it is the biggest natural disadvantage. We work to manage the disadvantage of this approach using virtual feature teams led by a project manager, technical lead, and qualification lead from one of the component teams. As described in Chapter 7, "Taming the Planning Beast," we also work to have clear priorities across the organization down to the feature level so teams working on the highest priority features can get the support across the component teams to finish the highest priority features first. This is working to a certain extent, but getting good feature ownership will continue to be a challenge we will need to manage, based on our decision to organize by components. This is one area where we struggle and will need to continue to improve by driving and emphasizing feature ownership through our metrics and expectations.

Somehow, the features still seem to come together well with good definition and good quality for a couple of reasons. We have a centralized team of system engineers (see Chapter 7) who oversee feature definition and who consult as issues come up throughout the life cycle of a requirement. This helps significantly in keeping a system/feature focus. Each team also tries hard to manage Work in Process (WIP) on an engineer-by-engineer basis so at any point in time, the "virtual feature team" we've created is a strong and focused team. If they are holding regular Scrum meetings, are passionate and focused on the feature at hand, and aren't overly distracted by other responsibilities, the feature can come together quickly and smoothly. Of course, those features with highest priority seem to be the ones that avoid technical problems or schedule delays because no one gets distracted by anything else.

You can tell this tension is strong in the organization through the regular discussions we have on this topic. For example, someone told the engineering director that we needed to change our organization to feature teams because he was not able to complete his objective in the last MM because the teams he needed were on higher-priority activities. The director pointed out that he felt this was fine because the PM was trying hard to drive closure on one of our lowest priorities. In this case, our approach was working as designed, and we had a frustrated PM because we were trying to drive too much work into the system.

In other cases, we have architects that think we are doing a poor job of feature ownership. In one case, although we have designated feature leads and kickoff meetings, an architect was questioning how well we do feature ownership and if it is really happening with every feature. This is a case where our organizational approach is working against us, and we need to do a better job of walking the talk and making sure we are measuring and driving ownership on the feature view that goes across organizational boundaries.

Some struggles aside, it has been almost magical to watch our virtual feature teams in action. We still form them frequently (virtually, not organizationally—with a project manager, a technical lead, a qualification lead, and a system engineer as the core team, plus all the developers from every collaborating team). When these teams get moving and are working on something high enough priority to be unobstructed, they might as well be an organization-based feature team. Everyone unofficially reports to the feature owner (project manager), and we've seen it happen numerous times that the teams get so passionate about what they're doing and on getting it finished that the collaboration and progress on the team is a wonderful sight. We'll continue finding ways to strengthen our virtual feature teams and get them happening more consistently; but for the foreseeable future, we're staying with our bias toward component quality and scalability that comes with the component team model.

Traditionally Managed Project Teams versus Self-Managed Scrum Teams

In its truest sense, a Scrum is a self-managed team driving ownership and delivery. This is analogous to the self-managed teams that were popular in manufacturing during the late 1980s and early 1990s, where management literally gets out of the way and the team self-organizes and works through everything on its own. Although it's never that black and white, there are definitely different approaches. Table 10.4 shows the advantages and disadvantages of traditional versus self-managed teams.

TABLE 10.4   Traditional versus Self-Managed Teams

Traditionally Managed Project Teams	Self-Managed Scrum Teams
Advantages: ■ Clear management line of accountability to delivery. ■ Clear ownership for driving coordination across teams. ■ Clear leadership for driving business success.	Advantages: ■ Highly motivated teams. ■ The team is more likely to make its own ideas successful than the manager's idea.
Disadvantages: ■ It is harder to get the team to own the success for the decisions or approaches. ■ It is more difficult getting the teams excited and engaged.	Disadvantages: ■ You can spend more time making sure you are doing self-managed teams right than making sure you are delivering on the business objectives. ■ Lack of clear lines of accountability.

It is quite hard to get 400+ people around the world to align and deliver anything all together, much less a very complex software/firmware system. To make this a reality, we leverage and depend heavily on our traditional team structure, with the whole management team very involved and driving things. The planning of the deliveries, distribution of work, executing to our priorities, and coordinating across teams requires a strong and fully engaged management team. Additionally, we have the pleasure of leading a very dedicated and highly motivated group of engineers. Therefore, we stuck with the more traditional approach to managing the teams. Maybe on a smaller scale the self-managed Scrum approach would work better, or in the case where a company was having difficulty getting the team to take ownership for the decisions. For us it felt like the change was not worth the complexity at this scale, and it was not an area where we felt we would get the biggest bang for our buck. The potential ideas for agile can be overwhelming and all consuming. This is a case where we made a conscious decision to go against the academic practice as we drove to large-scale agile.

Like other organizational decisions, we work to offset the disadvantages of this approach. First and foremost, we don't see that the manager's job is to tell the organization what and how to do its job in a command-and-control sense documented in some agile books. It is to clearly define the strategic directions and organizational priorities and then, working with the team, to get everyone driving in that direction. Next, it is to monitor progress and work with the teams to understand what is and what isn't working. The managers then help the organization improve where things are struggling. This often means making the bottleneck visible so we can optimize the organization toward helping the team that is struggling. Or it means getting the needed help from another team where dependencies exist. It could be working with the product owners to get clearer definition for a user story, or negotiating for a smaller feature load so they can catch up with some development debt. It could be working with the team to highlight and drive process changes that would make the organization more effective. It could be working with upper management to increase funding or capacity in that area so they are set up for long-term success. In any case, the role of the management team is to define the direction and then work with the team to help the team succeed.

Summary

Go ahead and organize your test and development teams however you'd like—there really isn't a right and wrong way. However, be conscious of the impacts and natural weaknesses of how you organize, and put processes, tools, or individuals in place to cater to the disadvantages of your chosen organization and help counterbalance the strengths.

Chapter 11

EFFECTIVE AGILE DEVELOPMENT ACROSS U.S. AND INDIAN CULTURES

As is apparent everywhere, organizations have started utilizing India for lowering engineering costs. We've done the same thing and would like to spend a few paragraphs discussing lessons learned in our experience together with our team in India. We have a very healthy experience now, but it took going through tough times to get where we are today. We hope sharing our experience will provide the information we wish we had before starting out.

Outsourcing overseas is straightforward for support type functions where one person needs to interact with the customer on one problem, and the process for resolution is fairly well known. But for R&D work involving far more uncertainty and innovation, there needs to be more focus on the quality of the engineers than on just the cost of the engineers. There are great engineers everywhere, but this aspect that is often found easily locally has to be specifically paid attention to when working remotely. We've found the cost per engineer argument starts to break down because the productivity delta between average engineers and the best engineers can be an order of magnitude and can easily offset the differences in cost per engineer.

Increasingly we're finding that India is a great opportunity to find good talent. India has invested in its businesses and educational system to develop software/firmware as a core competency. However, finding top talent regardless of location is difficult, and India is no exception. As a U.S.-based team, there were lots of lessons in learning how to effectively work with our team in India and overcome cultural differences. Being successful working across these cultural differences has required us to understand those differences and make a few adjustments to our approach. Our R&D teams in India are well qualified and getting more qualified by the year. They also are incredibly motivated to work very hard and do a good job.

In this chapter, we cover six lessons learned in integrating our development efforts with those of our Indian colleagues:

- Permission to Ask
- Ensure Time to Explore
- Have Small Wins First
- Exploit the Time Difference
- Take Time to Train—Always
- Remember a Team Is About People

Each of these lessons is reviewed in the sections that follow.

Lesson 1: Permission to Ask

From a U.S. perspective, we found we needed to make sure our Indian counterparts knew we expected them to ask questions. We helped them understand that doing so is not a sign that they are in any way less capable. We've found this is not a natural part of their culture, and it feels uncomfortable for them at first. Without asking questions, there's no way to know what's really needed or to check assumptions. We see this type of collaborative dialog happening continuously and naturally on our U.S.-based teams.

A key lesson was to ensure we gave *permission to ask*. We needed to let our India team members know that they need to keep us informed of any issues before they get big and out of control. At the management level, we meet regularly to get status updates and track progress. We make sure that at the lower levels of the organization, both sides are aligned on the content of the status so that the two teams agree and there aren't surprises. The constant feedback process and dialog enables us to see when we are drifting off the intended course in real time and make adjustments.

Lesson 2: Ensure Time to Explore

Another key learning was to allocate *time to explore*. We needed to give our development teams in both the United States and India time to learn about each other and come to some conclusions in their own time. As items have come up from discussions together, we've made sure everyone is aware of naturally occurring tensions; this helped the two worlds understand each other and work more closely together. For example, we had to recognize and address that some U.S. team members occasionally have concerns about job security and the extra work of bringing a remote team up to speed. Conversely, the India teams who have such a strong work ethic and brilliant minds struggle with the feeling of needing to prove themselves before being fully accepted and trusted to contribute effectively. A natural and powerful outcome of exploring is just getting to know each other. As soon as a person has a face, a personality, and a real connection, it's amazing how the natural tensions fade away (see Lesson 6 in this chapter about focusing on the people).

Lesson 3: Have Small Wins First

A key lesson was to *have many small wins*. We've found it best to start with small wins where we can get something done completely and well. Although it may not be the most exciting, it enables members of the team to start making a meaningful contribution right away. This had the advantage of having the India team demonstrate their contributions with small helpful tasks and build credibility instead of taking on big, complicated tasks where they might struggle. This is a key in any engagement, but it is even more important in distributed teams where engineers rely on less-direct communication methods like email and daily check-ins to stay synchronized. Just like in all of agile, undercommit and then overdeliver.

Trust is built on three things: competence, goodwill, and integrity. In this context, competence equals the ability to deliver; goodwill is created by speaking well of each other and showing respect; and integrity comes from doing what you say you'll do. In the U.S. culture, we tend not to doubt people's integrity, but rather, if a deadline is missed, blame competence.

After the team members had "proven themselves" and there were successes, larger tasks could be assigned with more accountability, allowing contributions in ever bigger ways. This probably seems counterintuitive to success, but for us, our U.S. culture tends to put a lot of emphasis on "prove yourself first" (competence first) to earn the proper respect and trust. Right or wrong, it's real, and we've found that this approach can help overcome that.

We've also extended this "small wins" idea by having our India teams use sprint objectives. It's amazing how this helps control what is committed to and also makes agreements and expectations clear and clean. This has provided focus and excitement as teams find the right balance of how much can be done in four weeks.

Lesson 4: Exploit the Time Difference

We *take advantage of the time difference*. At first, we naturally saw it as a burden and inhibitor to efficiency and collaboration. But in an agile environment, our responsibilities can be coordinated so that a change request can be fixed on one side of the planet, and then seamlessly tested much more quickly on the other. Because continuous integration and automated testing have been so much a part of our agile experience, the time difference means it's easy to provide 24-hour server/tool/build/test support when things go down or have problems. Or when competencies are equivalent, feature development, integration, and test can happen seamlessly through the day and night, increasing throughput and responsiveness significantly.

Lesson 5: Take Time to Train—Always

We always make sure now that we *take time to train*. Whether formal or via a mentor, we treat it as an extension of an existing team to start, not as the responsibility of an independent team. Over time, the independence and full accountability have come very naturally.

Lesson 6: Remember a Team Is About People

Finally, the *personal element makes all the difference* for us. Although it can be a significant investment, it has been totally worth having engineers visit back and forth during the early months of working together or when substantial changes occur in assignments or personnel. Then it isn't "a faceless someone from that other culture" we're working with, but a friend and cohort that has personality, a sense of humor, and known and understood strengths. When the expense of getting together directly is too much, we also do a lot of video-conferencing. We utilize HP's Halo Collaborative Studios, which offers a very immersive audio-visual experience that can help accomplish many of the purposes without the same disruption and expense. Our HP team has a significant investment in collaboration with India. The joint success truly began when everyone on both sides of the world got to know each team member as individuals and they became part of the collaborative working team.

We've also found that teams in India need to develop critical mass and plans so they can do all the first-level training for new employees on their own. When first starting up, this is a large cost, both in terms of travel and time away from home for many, and also in terms of mentoring new employees.

We believe this development model is not likely to be successful in a downturn in order to save costs by moving jobs overseas. We've found it's already challenging enough without adding in the element of "I may be training my replacement." So we started this offshore model when the economy was good enough and our business was expanding, not contracting, so that it's seen as a positive by helping remove bottlenecks, and there's motivation and excitement to make it work well.

Organizing for the Highest Leverage of Offshore Teams

We've discussed the lessons learned with offshoring. We also want to share how we organized in working with offshore teams to be the most effective for us. Like everything else, this has been a "learn as you go" process for everyone involved. We have adapted many times during the past several years and continue to adapt as we progress together. There is not a lot published on the "right" way to leverage offshore teams in large-scale agile development. The debate we typically have is around whether the offshore teams should be integrated with existing onshore teams or should operate as self-sufficiently and independently as possible. The pros and cons of each are listed in Table 11.1.

> **Note**
> As you'll see in the rest of this chapter, we ended up utilizing a combination of both of these organizational models.

TABLE 11.1   Offshore Team Organization

Integrated with Existing Teams	Self-Sufficient and Independent
Advantages: ■ Ability to ramp up new capacity and train new engineers ■ Ability to help quickly start adding value ■ Ability to leverage capabilities and move engineering capacity to assist the bottleneck ■ Opportunity to take advantage of time zone differences to make progress around the clock	Advantages: ■ Better ownership and stronger retention ■ Less need for coordination across time zones and sites
Disadvantages: ■ Communication across time zones and sites is more difficult ■ Less sense of ownership for work and contributions	Disadvantages: ■ Limited view of how to make the whole system work ■ Difficulty in adding capacity where required ■ False starts and potential impacts to architecture and quality if not overseen closely or if doing this too quickly before skill set/knowledge is sufficient

When we first started ramping up capacity in India, we had many ongoing debates about what kinds of work we could and couldn't give to our India teams if they were going to be successful. They really wanted complete ownership of things, which in many cases they weren't ready for. This resulted in several surprises at the end, where we had to jump in and help fix things. Over time, we transitioned this more to an approach where they were augmenting teams and really helping out versus arguing over who does what work. This happened at a time when all the teams were overloaded bringing up a new architecture, so any additional help was appreciated. The teams from India jumped in and started helping wherever they could and started building credibility, respect, and relationships with the U.S.-based teams.

We spent a lot of time bringing the engineers from India to the United States for training and relationship building, which helped immensely.

We did not spend much energy discussing which work should happen where, and up to this point it has naturally evolved. Currently, the team in India successfully owns leadership for one pillar/component. They have also taken ownership for releasing new features quarterly on existing products and responding to escalations by our sales force and support organization. They also continue to be extensions to and additional capacity for several existing U.S.-based teams. Our engagement is very successful in terms of the value the teams are providing the business. In addition, they are happy and engaged with their roles and responsibilities.

It was not clear to us or the team in India when we started that it would work out this well, but because we are on one branch/code base for new and released products, it makes a lot of sense that they need to play all these roles to be successful. They need the expertise they have developed in each of the component areas to enable them to own their new charter of releasing new features to the existing fleet. If they have a change request from the field or a new feature doesn't work on existing products, the in-depth relationship and experience they developed from their integration with existing teams enables them to work closely to make sure there is a solution that works across the product line. In fact, the initial plan when they took on the new charter of rereleasing existing products each quarter was that this would be a separate set of teams for them (versus their teams that "augment U.S.-based teams"). But very quickly, as they analyzed how to organize, they discovered that integrating these teams within India gave the most flexibility for supporting new feature development and product rereleases, and it generated built-in expertise sharing. And they can move people around from CPE work (supporting the existing fleet in the field) to new feature and new product work seamlessly as needed.

We had a hard time convincing their management team in the beginning, and it took a while for them to see the value. Currently they are happy with their charter and see how all the roles function together and help them provide value to the business. It has been exciting as the offshore teams have evolved and have been given complete ownership for certain areas, to watch them go from doing the work they are asked to do to truly looking for opportunities for improvement across the system in terms of improving scalability, quality, and efficiency/effectiveness in everything we do together. We knew we were starting to hit on all cylinders when in our meetings they were predicting overall needs and proactively offering plans to help.

As our India-based teams have continued to increase in experience, they have even continued to take on additional responsibilities, including some limited feature development. The critical thing has been to continue to increment in small steps and assure success before launching into larger initiatives.

Summary

What started out as a tentative working relationship has truly blossomed into a powerful competitive advantage in responding quickly to challenging problems. Teams have embraced the opportunity this arrangement provides and have learned to adapt to the challenges that come with crossing cultures and time zones. The most important thing to remember is to be flexible and adaptable—and focus on the people and relationships as you build trust together.

Chapter 12

THE RIGHT TOOLS: QUANTUM LEAPS IN PRODUCTIVITY

As far as our motivation for starting agile development, it was all about improving productivity, and in particular, improving feature throughput and code quality through increased developer productivity. We've already described the processes we changed to accomplish this, but this chapter is all about the infrastructure behind the processes. Although everyone spends a lot of time investing in code architecture for scalable, reusable software or firmware, it's not so natural to think about a scalable, reusable architecture for integration and build processes, for test harnesses and test execution, or for metrics collection and reporting. But where productivity is the focus, these are just as or potentially more important than the architecture for the code. They are the secret to achieving frequent high-quality code drops and to improving developer productivity. Two in particular that we've architected and created are just as fundamental and breakthrough as the automated build/integration system (IQ) we discussed in Chapter 5: our Common Test Framework (CTF) and the Virtual Machine Provisioning System (VMPS). They are largely what make it possible to do all the L0–L4 testing in an efficient way.

Beyond that, as we're sure you already know, tracking metrics on a frequent basis is critical because agile processes are so fast-moving that you can't rely on a manually produced weekly metrics report to watch where things are and where adjustments need to be made. Adjustments must be able to be made real-time. If a Scrum-Master is nothing else, he/she is a metrics watcher. That's the secret to seeing where impediments may be lurking and thus being able to move forward quickly to remove them.

When you start investing in build tools, integration tools, test tools, requirements tools, change request tools, and metrics tools, it turns out one of the critical needs is figuring out how they all work together. Do they link at all? Do they enable processes to work seamlessly together? Or are they clunky and inefficient with manual data transfer and synchronizing?

Finally, although it doesn't have anything to do with how we architected anything, there are some fundamental investments in "cool toys" for developers that companies often don't spend money on that both pay for themselves over and over in terms of investment versus productivity gains, but also make such a difference in the mood of the organization that the intangible portion of productivity also goes through the roof.

Common Development Environment

One of the big cultural changes we drove as part of our change process was blurring the line between developers and testers so that everyone felt they owned the quality of the code. In the past, the development role was very different from the testing role, which frequently drove different development tools. Therefore, when a change request was found, the developer frequently had to go sit with the tester to reproduce the failure on the test development box. This led to inefficiencies and slowdowns in the process. As part of our change process, we set the goal of making sure any test failure was reproducible on any development box anywhere in the world. *In fact, all of our developers and testers now have the same development images on all their boxes.* It sounds simple, but getting past the issue of different engineers getting different results takes a lot of waste out of the system. It used to be one of the most hated phrases in the organization was, "I don't know; it works on my box." This usually happened when one engineer was having problems with another engineer's code and was asking for help. This interaction was really demoralizing because the first engineer didn't want to waste any time helping because he felt the other engineer was not even adept enough to set up his development box correctly. The other engineer had to spend a lot of extra effort proving there really was an issue with the code where they needed help. When we moved to one development image for everyone, it completely removed this waste in the system. It also moved to an environment where testers and developers had the exact same setup. In the past, the testers usually had a unique setup for testing, so when there was a failure, the tester and developer would have to find time when they could get together and review the failures in the tester's environment. Now that everyone has the same image on their development boxes, it is doing a great job breaking down the walls between test and development. When new code breaks a test, the developer can easily reproduce it at his or her desk and quickly resolve the issue. In fact, we have even created a system for automatically sending an email to the developer when a test fails that includes a zip file with everything needed to reproduce the test failure immediately. This enabled developers to easily and efficiently take more ownership for the quality of their code.

Simulation and Emulation Environment for Automated Testing

Another key has been having a complete and capable system simulator. HP FutureSmart Firmware is embedded on a chip on a formatter board, which is the brains inserted into many product hardware platforms. To execute most of our tests every day, we have invested heavily in system simulation so we can develop and test without requiring early hardware prototypes for everyone, and so we can find and fix the majority of firmware issues before we ever touch a piece of hardware. In fact, if anyone finds a test failure while running on real product hardware, we consider it a "test escape," and we work quickly to increase our simulation/emulation capability or our test coverage on simulators/emulators to avoid it in the future. The simulator is a key enabler in making it possible to scale execution across dozens of hardware platforms. In previous programs, we haven't been able to scale test automation because we never had a system simulator that was capable of running all tests. Here are the basic definitions of what we mean by simulator, emulator, and product hardware:

- **Simulator**—A wholly software-based development and test environment that can run locally on someone's own development box or in our automated test farm. We want to find all code issues either in unit testing or in end-to-end simulator testing.

- **Emulator**—Similar to the simulator (shared code), but also includes the real controller board for the product so real timing, memory, and connectivity can be exercised. But the scan path and print path beyond the controller board hardware are still simulated (no actual scanner or print engine). Test libraries exist so that the same test can execute on either a simulator or an emulator.

- **Product hardware**—Even when we do have to run tests on real hardware due to simulation/emulation limitations, we still utilize automatic button pressing and sending of print jobs to the device wherever possible to make it hands off anytime we can. Having massive amounts of pure manual testing is the downfall of many large efforts to move to agile.

We have a full dedicated team doing simulator/emulator enhancements—for additional testability, productivity, and to assess ongoing needs for simulation as more complex features are developed. We used to deliver new products and features and only ask well into development what additional simulation support we needed. Now we talk about it and act on it as the very first thing and try to have the new capabilities in place just in time for when the rest of the organization needs to engage.

Test Architecture for Scalability: Common Test Framework (CTF)

Every test developer has to write just about as much code as any firmware developer. We decided from the start that we needed common libraries for all test developers to use to more efficiently and consistently write tests in an automated environment. We've invested in multiple engineers on a test tools team to add additional capabilities to this test framework for all test developers.

Even with this effort, it wasn't until a few years in that we realized that although we had many high-level technology architects overseeing the firmware architecture, we didn't have an architect overseeing CTF, and we were seeing scalability issues, performance issues, and reliability issues as we expanded it beyond its initial scope. We quickly transferred an experienced architect to this area and have now rolled out a newly re-architected CTF 2.0. This has dramatically improved test execution performance as well as scalability of the test framework, so it can be used not only for system-level tests, but also for lower-level subsystem and component test harnesses and libraries. We went into this effort planning to dramatically drive up quality and testing with automation. The only thing that has been consistent throughout our development process is that we have consistently underestimated the strategic value of our testing architecture, infrastructure, and coverage investments. If you are going to use automated testing and Continuous Integration (CI) to dramatically improve your productivity, you need to treat your testing investments as being at least as important, or even more important, than your development investments, which is a big cultural change for most organizations.

In developing our automated testing plan, we made a few mistakes that ended up being pretty painful to correct after we had a large amount of automated testing in place that had to be updated. Probably the biggest mistake was testing through the UI for most of our automated testing. As we got an architect in place, we realized we needed to transition away from UI-based testing for a couple of reasons. First, UI-based tests run very slowly, which limits the amount of testing that can be covered in each step of the deployment pipeline, even if you could afford the extra hardware. Second, because the UI is the part of the product design that changes most frequently, having UI-based testing can drive significant thrash into automated tests. The other area where we could have improved is better planning of our automated testing across the deployment pipeline. We selected tests for stage 1 and 2 based on what we thought would give us the best smoke test for that level, regardless of the time required for each test.

In hindsight, and after reading *Continuous Delivery* by Jez Humble and David Farley, we should have organized things a bit differently. For instance, because unit tests are very fast, we should have run every unit test in Stage 1. This would have provided the best coverage. It would also have helped drive the cultural shift to always keeping unit tests passing (if a unit test didn't pass Stage 1, the code would have been automatically reverted). We spent a lot of time trying to get the organization to embrace unit testing through reinforcing behaviors at the management level when we could have made it an automatic part of our process. There are a lot of other good ideas for designing automated tests to work across the deployment pipeline that are included in the *Continuous Delivery* book that we wish we had known before we started our journey. We highly recommend reading this book before you make any significant investments in automated testing.

Prior to HP FutureSmart Firmware, we attempted to do test automation, but two things that kept it from getting off the ground completely were 1) a limited system simulator that was designed for some teams but not all (again, we got too busy executing to make time/resources available to improving our simulation abilities); and 2) no commonality among test frameworks. Because every component team had different needs, we previously had different test frameworks for almost every team. That meant a lot of wasted duplicate effort, and it kept teams from sharing tests and test libraries or from being able to execute each other's tests easily during triage.

The Most Important Part of Test Automation: Virtual Machine Provisioning System (VMPS)

It's easy to let off a cheer when you get your first automated test written. Now your testing is hands free! But there's a problem: Who's going to kick off the test? And how often? And what if it is designed to run on multiple platforms (simulator plus emulator)? How do I find and schedule the equipment for the test run? And what if I have 10 products I need to run a test against?

You can have awesome test harnesses and thousands of automated tests, but to truly create a hands-off automated testing process, there must be a test farm and a scheduling algorithm/tool to kick off tests to execute in that test farm and match those tests with the right equipment they need to execute. There's no way in the world we could execute 200,000 tests per day without a scheduling tool to make all this happen. The test leads or test contractors would be able to do nothing else but kick off test scripts.

We developed a tool called the Virtual Machine Provisioning System (VMPS) to support our automated testing. Without trying to explain the full concept or architecture here, the whole approach is to have previously defined test sets (a group of tests, created and stored in HP Application Lifecycle Management (ALM)) automatically selected and put into a queue, matched with the right hardware, get the right firmware build to test with, launch it, monitor to make sure it's successful, write results back to a test result repository when the test set completes, and notify the right set of people if a test fails.

Figure 12.1 is a snapshot of how to set up a new job in VMPS. It's quite simple and straight-forward but still flexible enough to enable interval-based scheduling, time-based scheduling, or to trigger when a code change has occurred. It includes the capability to hold the job on error, or when it completes, the capability to prioritize against other jobs (for times when all test resources are consumed) and a place to list several parameters used for reporting (product, pillar, manager, and so on). You also specify where the test script comes from in HP ALM and who gets emails on failure (or always). There's another notification scheme tied in with this that emails anyone who made a code change in the current build as well; the current protocol we've established is that whoever is first on that list must take the lead in figuring out who caused the failure so they can revert their change and everyone else can recommit.

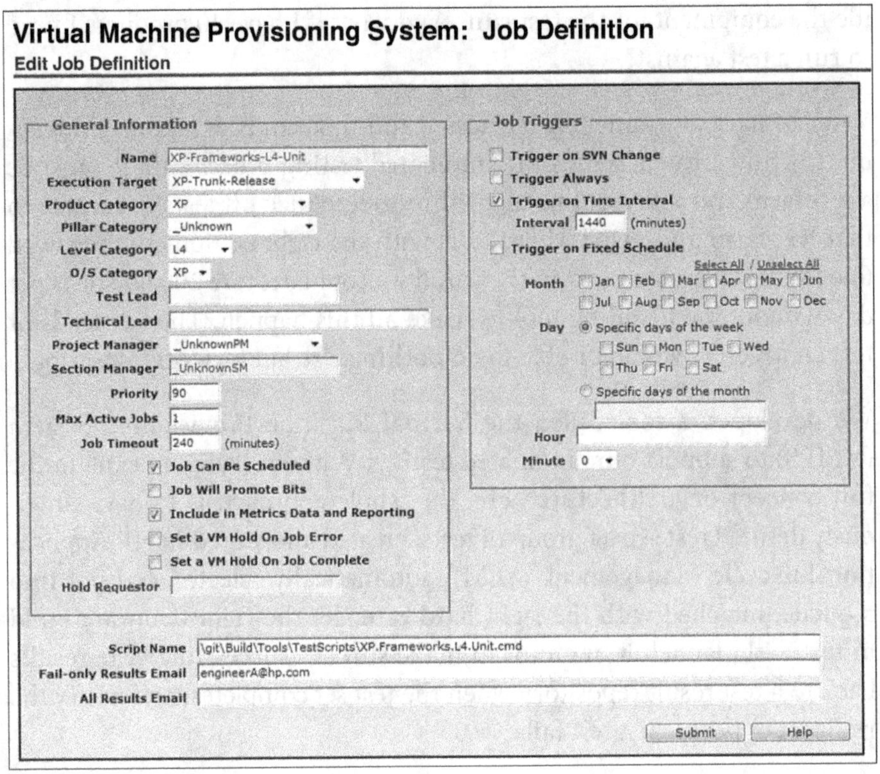

FIGURE 12.1   VMPS job definition

VMPS has rudimentary reporting built in. There are administrative reports for managing VMPS, including In-Flight Job Executions and system utilization. It also keeps a history of two weeks of results and has different reporting views (table, graph, timeline) that can be filtered by any of the specified parameters so you can see just your team's results, just the results for a given product, or filter on other parameters. The following figures present a few samples of the metrics output (see Figures 12.2 to 12.4).

Virtual Machine Provisioning System: Sample Timeline Report
All Recent Job Executions (Last 7 Days)

Completed Jobs

	Id	Result	Status	Start	End	Trigger	Version	Priority
	Mamba-Walkup-L2-B10.4-124188-43	Passed	47 of 47 Passed	01-03 02:53:24	01-03 06:28:46	TimeInterval	124188	91
	Mamba-Walkup-L2-B10.4-124186-42	Passed	47 of 47 Passed	01-02 14:26:15	01-02 17:51:18	TimeInterval	124186	91
	Mamba-Walkup-L2-B10.4-124185-41	Passed	47 of 47 Passed	01-01 15:56:16	01-01 19:25:18	TimeInterval	124185	91
	Mamba-Walkup-L2-B10.4-124184-40	Passed	44 of 47 Passed	12-31 17:55:02	12-31 23:12:39	TimeInterval	124184	91
	Mamba-Walkup-L2-B10.4-124182-39	Passed	47 of 47 Passed	12-31 03:12:23	12-31 06:44:18	TimeInterval	124182	91
	Mamba-Walkup-L2-B10.4-124180-38	Passed	46 of 47 Passed	12-30 16:30:07	12-30 20:44:14	TimeInterval	124180	91
	Mamba-Walkup-L2-B10.4-124176-37	Passed	47 of 47 Passed	12-29 14:24:04	12-29 17:48:07	TimeInterval	124176	91
	Mamba-Walkup-L2-B10.4-124175-36	Passed	47 of 47 Passed	12-28 15:38:28	12-28 19:03:13	TimeInterval	124175	91
	Mamba-Walkup-L2-B10.4-124174-35	Passed	47 of 47 Passed	12-28 01:44:09	12-28 05:16:17	TimeInterval	124174	91
	Mamba-Walkup-L2-B10.4-124172-34	Passed	47 of 47 Passed	12-27 16:25:00	12-27 20:06:25	TimeInterval	124172	91

FIGURE 12.2   VMPS results history

Virtual Machine Provisioning System: In-Flight Job Executions

Options	State	Job Id	Queued	Started	Completed	Hold Error	Hold Complete	Requestor	Priority
	Executing	Mamba-Cat-L2-B10.4-124188-350	01-03 14:00:05	01-03 14:00:13	01-03 18:00:13				92
	Executing	Mamba-Copy-L4-PaperHandling-B10.4-124186-271	01-02 19:12:58	01-02 19:19:41	01-06 03:19:41				110
	Executing	Mamba-DeviceManagement-L4-Emu-B10.4-124186-20	01-02 19:24:37	01-03 00:41:01	01-04 00:41:01				112
	Executing	Mamba-DigitalSend-L4-BC-Email-B10.4-124186-34	01-02 19:13:29	01-02 23:04:08	01-05 23:04:08				90
	Executing	Mamba-DigitalSend-L4-Features-B10.4-124186-34	01-02 19:13:44	01-02 23:19:17	01-05 23:19:17				90
	Executing	Mamba-DigitalSend-L4-ImagePreview-B10.4-124186-21	01-02 19:13:59	01-02 23:34:27	01-04 23:34:27				90
	Executing	Mamba-Imaging-S2F-A-L2-10.4-124188-47	01-03 02:54:36	01-03 02:54:45	01-04 02:54:45				91
	Executing	Mamba-Imaging-S2F-EMU-L4-10.4-124186-21	01-02 19:24:52	01-03 00:50:03	01-04 00:50:03				112
	Executing	Mamba-Imaging-S2F-L4-10.4-124186-33	01-02 19:14:52	01-03 23:49:34	01-03 23:49:34				90
	Executing	Mamba-Pdl-L4-PS-PaperHandling-Finishing-B10.4-124186-30	01-02 19:18:41	01-02 19:20:47	01-09 19:20:47				110
	Executing	Mamba-Print-L4Emu-Finishing-B10.4-124186-27	01-02 19:25:15	01-03 01:14:04	01-04 01:14:04				112
	Executing	Mamba-Print-L4Emu-Resets-B10.4-124187-30	01-02 21:00:03	01-03 11:55:41	01-04 11:55:41				112
	Deploying	Mamba-Print-L4Emu-Supplies-B10.4-124197-31	01-03 01:00:02	01-03 14:56:11	01-04 14:56:11				112
	Executing	Mamba-Security-L4-Permissions-B10.4-124186-32	01-02 19:21:58	01-02 19:35:33	01-04 11:35:33				110
	Executing	Mamba-WebContent-L4-Emu-1-B10.4-124186-16	01-02 19:25:30	01-03 03:30:38	01-04 03:30:38				112

FIGURE 12.3   VMPS active test job status

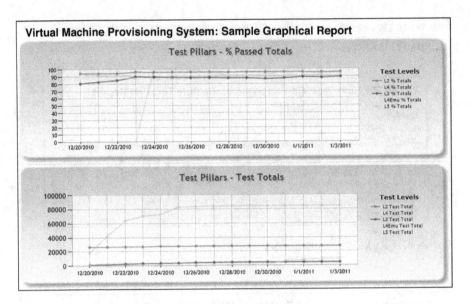

Virtual Machine Provisioning System: Sample Graphical Report

FIGURE 12.4   VMPS sample graph (test history)

Real-Time Metrics and Tracking

We've found it critical to have a common set of metrics that everyone tracks so all levels of the organization are on the same page. This helps drive priorities and alignment, including cascading objectives. It's easy to overdrive the system, so metrics are a tool used to have a conversation with the right people to help remove whatever barriers exist to getting on track. The old HP adage of "management by wandering around" is as alive and well in our organization as it ever has been anywhere. It's fundamental to everything we do. We constantly use the metrics to help us effectively ask the right questions of the right people across the organization, monitor the stress points, and not put too much work in the system.

We strive to use metrics within a given tool wherever possible instead of creating our own. We use HP ALM for requirements management, change request management, and test management, so we utilize its own graphs and reports for the most part for those three processes.

Note

HP Application Lifecycle Management (ALM) software (formerly QualityCenter) has a more holistic view of test data than VMPS because it includes all history, not just two weeks' worth, and it also includes any manual tests.

But there are times when it's nice to "push" data out to the right people in an email so they are more likely to look at it and manage to it. It's also key to integrate the metrics with the organizational reporting structure via LDAP lookup so you can have sum up/drill-down metrics for each level in the organization. Plus, it lowers the load on the actual tool usage if we offload reporting. We have an integrated "daily news" that goes out in email each morning, plus a web-based version of it that updates hourly. It combines text from the Scrum-Master (sprint objectives, upcoming milestones), metrics from HP ALM (requirements, change requests, tests), test execution metrics from VMPS, build and integration metrics from IQ, and code health metrics from the code repository in GIT into one dashboard view that keeps everyone on the same page quickly and easily.

Integrated Toolset

After several iterations with different vendors over the years, we now rely very heavily on all the linkages built into ALM to enable requirements-based testing, efficient change request submitting from test failures, and ties from our source code repository to ALM. We have built a few other linkages into ALM from VMPS and our metrics systems. We had some painful years of not having all these things linked together before we settled on this solution. It has made all the difference to have most of the integration be already available out-of-the-box.

We started out by creating a code architecture that scaled easily across products. What we missed is making sure our linkages from product requirements to tests were created so that it was easy to bring up all the right tests for new products. We are still working on fully utilizing the integration between requirements and tests for autoselecting all tests based on the requirements data. This will save significant non-value-added work we do today to manually set up new tests for every product. We have piloted an integrated solution for this and are now rolling it out to all teams.

Cool Toys Worth Investing In

We not only continually evaluate our processes to make sure we aren't being wasteful or inefficient, but we also evaluate our work environment to be sure the "tools of the trade" are as helpful as possible. Although they didn't come "standard issue" at HP, we made the decision to spend part of our R&D budget to get two things for every developer: a high-resolution 30-inch monitor and high-end noise-cancelling headphones. In the overall cost of running an R&D group, this is a pretty small expense, but you wouldn't believe what a difference it has made. When you think of the cost of an engineer, and then you figure out how much easier it is to develop and debug with twice as much screen space in a quiet environment, it makes you wonder why this sort of simple thing isn't done everywhere. When we first started with the large screens (because a lead architect kept telling us it was the most valuable real estate in the world), we thought it was worth a try because we were looking for anything possible to improve productivity. As we look back, thinking now of large monitors as the norm, it is hard to imagine how anyone could be as effective at development with smaller monitors.

We are constantly looking for new ideas or tools to improve developer productivity. Even though we are very large scale, we'd rather make breakthroughs in productivity ahead of hiring more engineers and making interfaces and communications more complex (plus, productivity tools are much more affordable than hiring additional engineers).

Summary

Happy engineers are productive engineers. It's worth the investment to staff a few centralized tool and infrastructure teams to analyze bottlenecks, listen to frustrations across the development and test organizations, and work tirelessly to improve things for them. These teams should consist of experienced, passionate engineers and managers that can effectively lead the organization along and drive forward on a regular basis to accomplish new breakthroughs in engineer productivity.

Chapter 13

REAL-WORLD AGILE RESULTS: HP FUTURESMART FIRMWARE

Up to this point, we have walked through the fundamental changes in our development process and architectural approaches. We have also showed what we changed to reduce cycle time, eliminate waste, and produce other improvements. As you can see in the summary graphic in Figure 13.1, we changed almost everything in our architecture, process, and development environment. What we have not made clear yet is whether this is just an interesting engineering experiment or a significant breakthrough for the business. Why should you care, and why should any business leader of a technology company care? Are the business results significant enough to justify the investments and the journey to change the development processes and architecture? The chart in Figure 13.1 summarizes the points we've discussed in the prior chapters about the key parts of agile and lean development that have made a difference for us.

The following sections in this chapter describe the business benefits that we have realized as a result of implementing these large-scale agile changes: resources moved from overhead to innovation, higher developer productivity, and improvement in current product support.

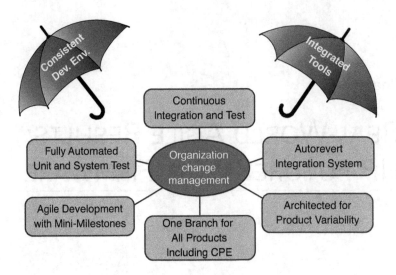

FIGURE 13.1 FW development changes—key advantages

Resources Moved from Overhead to Innovation

Here's a business-focused summary of the differences in the bottom line resulting from all our large-scale agile improvements. If you look at the development cycle time and cost drivers, you can see we made significant improvements in taking non-value-added time and work out of the system:

- **Code integration (10% → 2%)**—The resources doing integration are not doing manual processes now as they were before. They are a small, dedicated team proactively building new tools for improvement. They also are an expert resource to help on occasion where needed if large integration problems or infrastructure problems occur. We have some of the most highly regarded engineers in this space, continuing to push forward toward even more autorevert concepts.

- **Detailed planning (20% → 5%)**—This is primarily our full-time system engineers, plus part-time from the technical leads on each team who help review feature designs for feasibility and assure architectural integrity as we make trade-offs. These resources are not being used for cost or schedule estimation, but for better feature definition and proactively building relationships with software/firmware demand generators (marketing, serviceability, manufacturing, and so on). This is key to making "undercommit/overdeliver" possible.

- **Porting (25% → 15%)**—We do still have pockets of porting going on in the code, but continue to drive it down through challenging every time we have to make changes unique to a given product. It has been critical to put passionate engineers into certain roles to oversee where we are with architectural integrity to maintain what we've achieved and continue to the next level.

- **Current product support (25% → 10%)**—At first we were going to keep current product support directly in the same teams with new product/feature work. But we realized that it would be hard to have a quick response process to field escalations and still be able to make progress on future initiatives. So, we created a small, dedicated team for this. However, they use the same processes and the same code as all teams, with very tight alignment and collaboration with everyone else, so expertise can be put wherever needed to quickly respond to real customer needs. And this current product support team also takes over qualifying all new features on products already in the market. The whole idea of HP FutureSmart Firmware is to have a uniform flow of new innovation not just to new products, but to a fleet of existing products as well.

- **Resources spent on running tests (15% → 5%)**—We had a huge army of technicians running manual tests. We still have more manual tests than we would like, but we continually work to drive it down.

- **Value proposition/customer differentiation (~5% → ~40%)**—To date, most of this bucket has been spent getting the full architecture in place, including all fleet compatibility features. We're still playing catch up in some critical areas as well, but as we look at where we are spending our time now and going forward, we're starting to deliver on the innovative feature lists the demand generators want that will propel our products and solutions to an even greater leadership position in the market and dramatically reduce overall manufacturing and support costs of the business.

NOTE: Notice the "after agile" percentages don't add up to 100%. The remaining effort is in areas we weren't investing in previously. 3% are working on improved test tools, harnesses, and simulation/emulation. 10% are focused on writing new automated tests (higher coverage, new features, closing test escapes). The final 10% do daily triage of failures that come out of now daily regression testing (a lot more test data to process!). We're now embarking on a "10x tester productivity improvement" initiative (getting rid of intermittency, enabling auto-test selection for new products, test sparsing, and so on) like we did for developers so that we can continue moving more resources into innovation.

- **Cycle time for developer change to feedback for a complete testing cycle (2 months → 1 day)**—We've been dramatically successful in reducing our overhead and being able to refocus the organization on delivering innovation. But let's not stop there. There are other things that matter to the business. Remember, even if agile is fun and exciting, it's worthwhile only if it impacts the business results. What else does your business care about, and how is it faring?

R&D and Developer Productivity

We started out talking about how firmware had been a major constraint for the business for 20+ years. We tried spending our way out of the problem and that didn't work. So we set off to engineer a solution to improve developer productivity by 10 times and unleash the Product Roadmap (keep firmware off the critical path of introducing as many products/solutions as the business desires), at the same time needing to dramatically reduce our development costs. The results speak for themselves:

- From 2008 to the present, we reduced overall development costs by 40%.

- The number of programs under development increased by 140%.

- Development costs per program went down 78%.

- Firmware resources now driving innovation increased by 8 times (5% to 40%).

This shows at a high level we made significant breakthroughs in the costs required to support new product introductions. The overall spending went down with a dramatic increase in the number of products supported. One of the biggest breakthroughs from our perspective is that we have created a development engine that effectively supports a large number of engineers either fixing change requests or adding features to a main branch that we can keep stable. Add a feature or fix a change request once, and it's instantly propagated and tested against the whole fleet of products. It took significant changes across the system, but the results are dramatic. It addresses the evolving customer requirement of needing consistent features across new and old products. When customers buy HP, they know it is a safe investment because their hardware can stay the same but the firmware can evolve and change to support their evolving business needs.

This firmware breakthrough in terms of customer value was so significant the business decided to brand it *HP FutureSmart Firmware* and invest in marketing this capability. There's a great YouTube video that gives an overview of the real customer and business impact of FutureSmart Firmware:

http://www.youtube.com/watch?v=j2AFoRzUeUA.

It was all enabled by the development engine that dramatically improved developer productivity. The term "developer productivity" can be somewhat subjective. Some in the organization will say we hit the 10x improvement goal. Others will question if it was really a full 10x; but either way, you can see in Figure 13.2 that it was a big breakthrough in the productivity of everyone involved. By the measures we've looked at, we definitely hit it: number of builds per day, time to build, time to test, time to address a change request, time to integrate, lines of code per developer, and number of features per sprint.

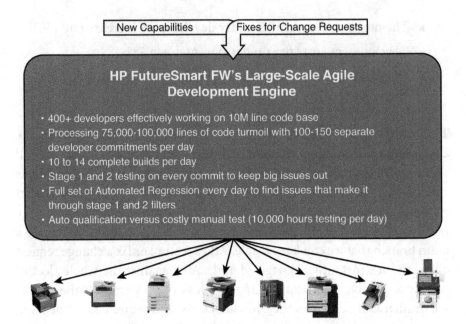

New Capabilities

Fixes for Change Requests

HP FutureSmart FW's Large-Scale Agile Development Engine

• 400+ developers effectively working on 10M line code base
• Processing 75,000-100,000 lines of code turmoil with 100-150 separate developer commitments per day
• 10 to 14 complete builds per day
• Stage 1 and 2 testing on every commit to keep big issues out
• Full set of Automated Regression every day to find issues that make it through stage 1 and 2 filters
• Auto qualification versus costly manual test (10,000 hours testing per day)

FIGURE 13.2   Breakthrough capacity for integrating code and deploying across fleet

Improvement in Current Product Support

The improvement in developing new products is dramatic, but we also had issues with being able to support the current products in the field with new firmware. The costs of supporting the existing fleet had grown to 25% of our overall spending. We were having a hard time adding features to the existing fleet so customers could have a consistent experience over products bought over time. We were also having a hard time addressing change requests submitted from the field. It is still early to fully demonstrate the results of these changes because the new products with HP FutureSmart Firmware are still quite new to the market. But in our first pass, we were able to add six times more features and fix more than six times the number of customer change requests while spending less than half the costs per product of a typical post-introduction release on the old architecture.

Summary

During the transformation, we were typically so caught up in the four-week sprint delivery and setting ongoing incremental objectives that we didn't take time to look back and realize how far we'd come. In taking time to reflect back and calculate the real-world impact over a four-year transformation, it was so worth the investment and the challenge of managing so much change. We encourage you to take time to look back at regular intervals and measure your success in terms of what's truly important to the business. Then spend some time communicating this information and celebrating the successes in this business context. It boosts morale but also helps assure ongoing investment and belief in the power of large-scale agile by business leaders up the management chain.

Chapter 14

CHANGE MANAGEMENT IN MOVING TOWARD ENTERPRISE AGILITY

The other area (besides how we're organized, and how we do project management) where Jim Highsmith, an executive consultant with Thought-Works, encouraged us to provide more clarity is around the process of change management and how things work differently after the transformation. We started out with a goal of dramatically improving productivity and getting firmware off the critical path for the business for the first time in more than two decades. We went after changing our architecture to address changes in our customer expectations and radically changing our development processes to eliminate work that was not directly contributing to our value proposition. This took some time and a lot of effort, but what we started to find after the transformation is that the change was starting to have a broader impact on the business. It was like the firmware transformation was a splash in the pond and we were seeing the unintended ripple effects across different groups.

The firmware quarterly releases rolling new features into both new and existing products began impacting other parts of the organization. This included other R&D groups, including the software driver teams, the HP WebJetAdmin team (HP's enterprise printer management tool), third-party solutions, as well as the qualification teams that do final system qualification across the full HP solution. Many of these groups were already doing their own brand of lean or agile, but the whole thing didn't quite match because of key differences in how each group worked its processes. A new initiative is now just forming that is much broader than firmware to actively manage and improve more and more of the enterprise by moving to agile. It has also started affecting groups not directly involved in R&D. Marketing started changing their whole approach from driving the business from a product focus to a more product line and fleet approach. This, in turn, has had an impact on product and hardware teams who have been the sole integration and business focus for many years. All back-end processes of product generation that used to be "once-only per product" and very waterfall in their approach suddenly had to start adapting to the new reality of product content changing quarterly (documentation, service/support, marketing/sales).

Although it was not at all intentional, the business impact of transforming the firmware capabilities and process along with removing a long-standing bottleneck started leading the organization toward what Jim Highsmith would call "Enterprise Agility."[1] This chapter describes the exciting opportunities as well as the challenging impacts that came out of the working relationships of our R&D group with the rest of the organization, including system qualification, product program teams, and non-R&D product generation groups. With a reflection into this change management across the organization, we also reflect back on how we handled the challenges of change management, even within our FutureSmart Firmware organization.

Impacts on Other R&D Groups and System Qualification

The transformation of firmware development and capabilities had unintended implications across the different R&D organizations because firmware is just one part of HP solutions. The firmware has to work with

---

1. Adaptive Leadership "Accelerating Enterprise Agility," whitepaper by Jim Highsmith.

other components, such as the software drivers and HP WebJetAdmin across the fleet. When new capabilities are added quarterly, we need to make sure we can access the capability from the driver or configure it via HP WebJetAdmin or the embedded web server on the device where it makes sense. This led us to transitioning to a fleet release focus, not just for firmware but for our entire set of solutions. We are now driving all these components at a fleet level in terms of a prioritized set of requirements and a coordinated delivery. This coordinated delivery is now for both new and released products, which greatly increased the demand on our final system qualification team. The team has responded to this challenge with some creative and unique approaches. First, instead of just thinking about qualifying each product, it now uses a fleet qualification plan for all products in the window. Each window consists of a manifest that includes the revision of the release for each component. The system qualification team then takes the drops of the components in the manifest and spreads the testing across all the products for a system qualification. The team has also gone to a slice-based test model where it tests end-to-end solutions across all the assets early and works to get all the changes requests resolved before moving to the next slice to help reduce the Work in Process (WIP) across the broader system.

Impacts on Product Program Teams

The next group impacted by the transformation beyond the firmware developers was the product program teams. They are responsible for understanding the target market and driving everything required for the products to be successful. This transition was especially difficult for them because although it had a significant impact on their programs, they had limited control over the decisions or implementations. In essence, they were sitting back, waiting on a re-architecture they had not requested. At the same time, the schedule was not on time, and the firmware team was not ready to make firm commitments to all their "must" features two years in advance. They were used to being very much in control and running the business, so this change was very frustrating.

We started the change management process by holding weekly meetings with all the product program managers and their management team to review the status of the firmware development. The meetings started out quite contentious with a lot of frustration, but over time the product program teams starting understanding how we were managing the development and tracking the progress. It also gave them a chance to prioritize things that were blocking their programs. They were invited to every firmware checkpoint and had good visibility into all our metrics. Although this did not address all the frustrations during the transition, it did help with the change management process to bring them along on the journey. They now understand how we are managing the programs, and they are starting to see the value of the transformation.

The move to one branch of code for all products, combined with customers changing their focus to consistent features across the fleet, led to a big shift for the organization of the product teams. In the past, firmware, software, and WebJetAdmin would go to each product team meeting to collect all the "must" and "high want" features from each group and then answer to each team what they could deliver. There were some efforts to coordinate bit releases for products in the same time window, but it was still very product driven (see Figure 14.1).

After the transformation, this has changed to where each component is treated more as a fleet asset that provides code drops to the products. This is a big change where there is one "product owner" in marketing that is responsible for providing a clear set of priorities for firmware. The marketing leads for the different product programs can submit new ideas and request priorities, but one person is responsible for looking across everything and providing the fleet answer for the business. This has been a big change for the product teams and marketing, but over time they are getting used to the new approach. It has also led to a fleet release model where all the components are released and tested together on a regular rhythm on the whole fleet of products (see Figure 14.2). The product team now just aligns to take the fleet release that works best for its manufacturing release.

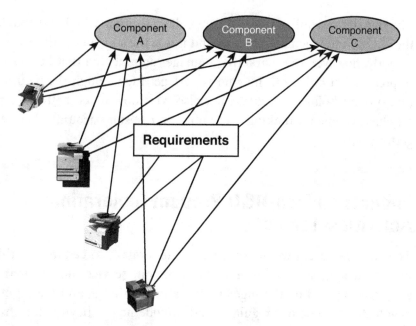

FIGURE 14.1   Began our journey with product-driven releases

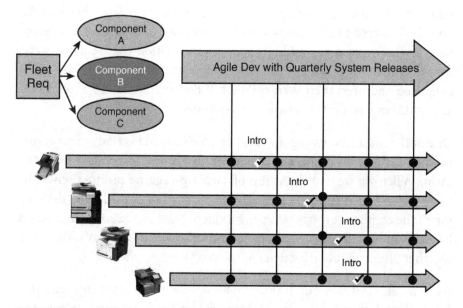

FIGURE 14.2   Currently trending toward enterprise agility with fleet releases and system qualification

The transition requires close and open dialog with marketing throughout the change management process, and it was initially met with resistance; recently, however, the marketing manager commented that he was truly impressed not only with how far we are getting through the request list (the product/solution backlog) but also with how much better our process has become for making trade-offs and decisions around what we are getting.

Impacts on Non-R&D Product Generation Activities/Teams

The other key areas where we were unintentionally forced to start thinking about agile are end-user documentation, service/support manuals and training, and marketing/sales literature, training, and messaging. If new features come out regularly and provide new behaviors for already released products, it's necessary to make sure that everyone thinks about the impact on them. It would be cost prohibitive to roll hardcopy documentation multiple times per year—not to mention that the material already delivered to customers would be very out-of-date. So these teams have started separating out key product information that remains static over the life of the product from common solutions that are always being enhanced and need their own agile set of deliverables. With a lot of creative thinking, so far things are progressing well.

One of the most interesting observations we've made is that teams across product generation appreciate a regular rhythm with product development. When we were at the whim of each zig-zagging product schedule, there was no such thing as a consistent rhythm of planning or delivery for all the common groups we've mentioned. Now, as the solution releases become more and more predictable and on time, the organization can, together, think about efficiencies at the next level.

As you can see from our transformation, when you start to make this fundamental change in a large enterprise, it tends to ripple across the system. We would recommend starting small and showing results before thinking about the broader impacts across the organization. However, after a transformation this large starts gaining momentum, you probably want to consider the interfaces between the agile groups and the more traditional parts of the business.

Where to Draw Boundaries with Coordinating Organizational Agility

As you can see from all the previous comments, this enterprise agility can quickly start rippling across the business. The benefits for component teams of coordinated fleet releases are great. The efficiencies for final qualification across the fleet are wonderful. Also, the peace of mind our customers get knowing that all the different versions of components have been qualified together is compelling. The challenge though, is that the more things you try to group together and qualify as a system, the more complex the process becomes to manage. The key we are starting to learn is that there is a balance between the efficiencies of enterprise agility and the system complexities that drive you away from the agility you set off to achieve. We are still early in the process of finding the right balance points, but it is clear that if the fleet release approaches are driven to extremes, you can start violating one of the basic principles of the lean/agile approach:

> **Reduce overhead and waste (keep it simple).** *If agile practices are adding more overhead to planning and development activities than you previously spent on them, it isn't agile.*

The system qualification group we work with recently introduced us to Dean Leffingwell's new book, *Agile Software Requirements*. The name of the book doesn't let on that it also captures a lot of insights into enterprise scalability and the concept of solution release trains, and how to manage them together. We've only just begun to work through both the benefits and challenges of taking large-scale agile to this cross-functional level, so we don't have a lot of insights or feedback yet. But we're sure learning as we go.

Change Management of the HP FutureSmart Firmware Transformation

We should point out that although the picture we paint of HP FutureSmart Firmware all sounds good in hindsight, getting the firmware organization to where we are today was a difficult transition across a large organization, and there was significant resistance to the change at several different points. The transition started out by combining three R&D labs and converging to the new code base, which was not a popular decision for many people across the organization. We also had difficulties meeting schedules as we converted the business to this completely new architecture. Pile on top of that the fact that we were moving to a completely new approach to firmware development, and as you can imagine, there was a lot of consternation in the organization. It is only now that the new architecture and approach has been out for a while that the organization as a whole is starting to appreciate the benefits and broader impact of the transformation.

It all started with the firmware development processes and objectives. The team had been working on firmware for HP LaserJet Printers for a long time and felt there was a better way of doing things. As described in the earlier chapters, we started with cost/cycle time drivers along with architectural changes. These chapters describe the technical changes but do not describe all the organizational change management required for the developers to start working differently. In the beginning, it was a big change for most of the developers that had been contributing firmware to a successful business for a long time. The idea of running a full set of regression tests every night, working off of one main code branch, having a common development environment, or expecting developers to write their own unit tests were pretty foreign concepts that were met with organizational resistance. When schedules would get tight, engineers would frequently bring up questions like, "When are we going to quit wasting time with unit testing and one main code branch and get back to the good old ways of driving schedules?" We would frequently have to point out that we were staying the course because, although the old way may have been quicker for writing code, the new approach was required to develop a supportable software/firmware platform.

We also had to start putting in different metrics to track and manage in order to show we were serious about changes in expectations. For example, we did not have a good test coverage tool for unit tests early on, so we started with a very simple approach that measured the lines of unit test code (T) in a component and the number of lines of firmware code in the component (C). We then divided these two numbers to establish a very rudimentary coverage metric called "T/C" to track components with poor coverage. We did not establish a goal for this metric but just used it to have conversations and ask questions. Early on, some components had very few unit tests, and some ended up with more lines of test than code.

Any engineers who had not bought into the vision ended up with T/C metrics at or close to zero, which led to discussions around resetting expectations. There were also engineers on component teams that were very passionate about unit tests and created good coverage. They would always make sure all the unit tests were passing before they checked in any code. In addition, other engineers on these teams who did not understand the value of unit testing would make changes that unknowingly broke unit tests from another team but check in their code anyway. This led to a high degree of frustration on these component teams because the unit test champions always had to clean up code from nonbelievers before they committed code. This is not a workable solution for making a transition. You need everyone on board with peer pressure and management helping to reinforce the expectation. It also helps with change management to capture and share stories on how the unit tests had done a good job of catching a big problem early and saving an engineer a lot of valuable time. In the end, changing behavior at the engineering level requires a clear understanding of the business strategy or vision, management championing the change, and metrics to track where the system is slow to adopt, because the platform is only as strong as the weakest code. It's also important that the metrics are used as "conversation starters" as described in Chapter 5, "The Real Secret to Success in Large-Scale Agile," instead of big sticks.

However, situations exist where individuals prefer their familiar, comfortable way of working and will push back on change. While not everyone can or has to be a leader in the agile movement, at some point everyone has to understand when a decision has been made to change the direction and that it's time to get on board. Having tools to help direct processes helps a lot, but sometimes it's better to help someone find another position in a more traditional environment in the company if they aren't comfortable with or adapting to everything new.

Change management never goes away, either. The best way we know to make it go well is one of the fundamental principles we brought up in Chapter 1, "Agile Principles versus Practices": "Practitioners should define agile/lean practices." The HP FutureSmart Firmware teams all actively participate in making things better. Instead of upper management stating an edict and making everyone follow it, if someone identifies inefficiency in how we do things, we change it if it makes sense and doesn't have other negative trade-offs. Our processes and tools have become just as agile as our development work, which is a key to success.

Summary

We did not start into this agile transformation thinking about the impacts or opportunities with all our product generation partners. But it has been important to acknowledge that it creates challenges for others, and to listen and learn and adapt to avoid suboptimizing for just our group. It has been rewarding to see the opportunities that have come up and been embraced to truly take advantage of "enterprise agile" and start seeing even larger business impacts when the end-to-end organization starts practicing agile. Change management is all about looking out for the other guys and thinking about their perspective as you migrate your processes. At the enterprise level, change comes more slowly and requires significantly more buy in. We've ended up stepping back several times and working closely with affected partners to help them see "What's in It for Me?" (WIIFM).

Chapter 15

DIFFERENCES IN OUR PERSPECTIVE ON SCALING AGILE

Looking back on our journey, it feels like our background caused us to take a somewhat different perspective on scaling agile to the enterprise than most organizations, which in hindsight was quite helpful. When we started out, we did not have much experience with agile, but we had a lot of experience doing development in a large enterprise. In the latter phases of getting this book published, we started getting lots of feedback from the agile community and spent time reading and learning more from their experiences. In hindsight, we probably should have spent more time up front getting involved with the agile experts to avoid having to learn as many things through the school of hard knocks. But our budget was tight, so we couldn't afford to bring in consultants, and we were so busy we didn't have time for much reading. As we engaged with other agile practitioners in industry, we found that most involved in scaling agile started with small agile teams and then scaled them up. Our whole experience was the other way around: W were already large-scale, and we adopted agile directly with 400 developers across three continents.

This chapter highlights the details of how our perspective was different from most efforts to scale agile, and how that unique perspective drove our focus areas, including the power and importance of a well-oiled deployment pipeline, a transformed planning mindset, an embrace of the uncertainties of software, and the critical nature of enterprisewide sprint planning and tracking.

A Difference in Perspective

As we look back at what we did differently in our agile transformation compared to many others who have adopted agile, it can be summed up by a difference in perspective. Are you trying to enable the efficiencies of small agile teams in an enterprise? Or are you trying to make an enterprise agile using the basic agile principles? There is not a right answer, but it is a question worth pondering as you start thinking about your own journey.

The approach to how to make empowered agile teams scale across the enterprise is covered very well by Dean Leffingwell's books, *Scaling Software Agility: Best Practices for Large Enterprises* and *Agile Software Requirements: Lean Requirements Practices for Teams, Programs, and the Enterprise*. He has done an excellent job describing all the details of how to make this work and has consulted with many organizations that have had success with this approach. They are both must-reads for any enterprise organization considering an agile transformation.

The approach we took is fundamentally different, probably because we were too naïve to know any better—and also because we didn't start small-scale agile first and then have to scale it. We were already large and complex when we adopted agile, so our experience was really about making agile work at a large scale versus scaling agile. So, we can't comment too much on the typical "how to scale agile for the enterprise" approaches in the industry. However, we believe our experience and the business results we demonstrated at least make it worth your consideration before you start your own journey. Also, in hindsight, for us and others we have discussed this with in the agile community, it is hard to imagine getting enterprise agility without some key agile fundamentals in place.

Focusing on Agility Rather Than Team Operations

The fact that we had a unique perspective started becoming more obvious as we had more people reviewing the book. There were frequent questions about how we started our teams, how we used coaches, how we got the organization signed up for a big agile initiative, and how we changed the roles for the management team as we moved toward agile. It made us realize that we did not really spend much time on these questions or approaches. We instead focused on the following type of questions for applying the principles of agile on a large scale:

- *How can we integrate early and often?*
  This question caused us to focus on large-scale Continuous Integration right from the beginning.

- *How can we create code that is always close to releasable?*
  Asking this got us to focus early and create a large-scale automated testing system integrated into our deployment pipeline.

- *How can we re-engineer our enterprise planning process to do it with a minimal investment?*
  This drove us to create a prioritized backlog with low-overhead estimation.

- *How can we keep the right short-term focus and know we're making significant progress?*
  This question helped us focus on managing WIP and driving continuous improvement with MM objectives and the iterative approach to agile management.

We did have different teams experimenting with agile techniques for their planning and tracking. The efforts ranged from full on Scrum with burndown charts and daily stand up meetings to teams that took a more traditional planning and tracking approach. We did not spend much time working with teams to influence what method they used. As far as we were concerned, as long as we were able to hit our four-week sprint (MM) objectives, how teams chose to manage the details of their piece of it was totally up to them. There was an effort to have all the different teams break the requirements into two to four weeks' worth of work so we could estimate capacity and expectations around automated testing with frequent integrations, but the teams were left with a lot of flexibility to choose what worked best for them. It is not clear that the teams using the full recommended Scrum approaches were more effective than other teams, because each team worked to make its approach successful. Therefore, some of the rigors around how the teams operate feel like more of a second-order effect versus changes to the automated testing, continuous integration, and enterprise planning, which had a bigger impact. Of course, improvements can be had by running the teams better, but from our experience, if you fix the other problems first, you are better set up to have the teams succeed.

This observation does not mean our approach was correct; it just feels like it is enough different that it is worth pointing out. To be fair, because we have not spent a lot of time focused on optimizing the operation of the teams, we are probably not in the best position to be offering an opinion. However, we achieved what we believe are significant business results, and it is hard for us to imagine doing large-scale agile development without addressing the previous areas we highlighted first.

Changing the Deployment Pipeline

Creating an enterprisewide efficient deployment pipeline integrated with large-scale automated testing feels like a must for large software projects. It supports integrating early and often and helps in quickly pinpointing the root cause of test failures down to the developer—or at least a small group of developers that are part of a specific build, which can be hard to find in a large organization. It is also key to keeping the code close to being ready for release, enabling working closely with customers on the minimal viable product and getting fast feedback on the product. For a large enterprise, this type of effort is probably best done as a centralized effort rather than an aggregated effort of several separate teams. Also, after it is in place enterprisewide, you have a solid development environment for the teams.

Embracing the Uncertainty of Agile

The second major shift that we believe is important to start at the enterprise level is transforming the approach and mindset around the planning process. This can be done as an aggregate of the teams, but we think it makes more sense to first create an enterprise approach for the teams to work within. The first step of this transformation is changing the mindset of the organization to appreciate the inherent uncertainty of software development. Software is problematic in that there is so much discovery work, it can't be successfully scheduled very far into the future. The organization needs to learn to accept that managing software is very different from managing other things that are much more deterministic, such as mechanical, electrical, or civil engineering work. This is a downside of software, and the whole agile movement has been created to address this weakness. The upside that needs to be appreciated is the flexibility inherent in software or firmware that can be changed at the last minute before a product introduction, released after the product released with upgrades, or be sold as a software service that can evolve daily with continuous delivery. The organization needs to change its mindset from fighting these inherent software traits to using them to its advantage. Instead of investing more and more to try to get accurate long-range estimates, organizations need to make the agile mental shift of exploiting uncertainty and flexibility as advantages in becoming more nimble. As in Judo, where you use the force of your opponent's attack to your advantage, the organization needs to accept the inherent characteristics of software and use the agile principles to move forward. If the organization doesn't make this mental shift at the enterprise level, the teams will be fighting an uphill battle.

At the enterprise level, the planning process also needs to provide lightweight, long-range forecasting tools to help drive capacity planning and prioritization processes for big long-term projects. This process needs to accept that in software, resources are the least flexible leg of the iron triangle. In reality, it is easy to go down in resources, but it is difficult to grow because it can take three to six months to get developers up to speed and productive in a new code base. Therefore, there needs to be a process at the enterprise level to plan what type and how much capacity is required over time and to smooth the peaks and troughs. This could come from an aggregation of the separate plans developed by the empowered agile teams, but we think it is best to start with an enterprisewide approach.

Enterprisewide Tracking and Incremental Improvements

The third major shift is creating an enterprisewide process for tracking progress and making continual improvements. We used the MM process for setting and adjusting goals each month. This led to a set of cascading objectives for tracking and monitoring progress daily during the iteration. We also used the agile management approach described in Chapter 5 for continually trying to understand what was working and where we needed to make improvements at the enterprise level; we were constantly taking advantage of what we were learning each iteration so we could adapt our processes and make adjustments for the next iteration.

Summary

Our hypothesis is that after you have created a solid deployment pipeline, helped the organization to embrace the inherent characteristics of software, developed an enterprise-level continuous improvement process like agile management, and created an enterprise planning process, **then** you will have the fundamentals in place for an agile enterprise. The team approach would then have an ideal environment in which to thrive.

The traditional approach of scaling agile teams in the enterprise comes up with approaches to address these fundamentals, but it also includes lots of organizational change that can be difficult to achieve and that takes a long time in a large organization. We also believe, based only on our singular experiment, that organization and team changes are a second-order effect. It is worth thinking about both paradigms and researching the options before choosing what would work best for your organization, but we thought it was worth pointing out the differences because our approach was different from what we perceive is the more common approach to scaling agile into the enterprise.

Chapter 16

TAKING THE FIRST STEP

So what do you think of our experiment? For us, it's been a wild but wonderful ride, full of passion and invention. We're not only doing large-scale agile development with quite amazing productivity numbers (at least compared to where we were; we haven't done any external benchmarking), but in such a way that a large, dispersed organization is empowered to truly act like a fluid set of small teams, working seamlessly without boundaries in delivering leading-edge technologies, products, features, and productivity tools. And we are doing it in a fun and positive environment. Although your business objectives, and thus the agile principles and practices you choose, may be completely different than ours, hopefully this real-world example has been a help to you—and will soon be a help to your organization.

On a recent India trip, one of the teams we met with listened very attentively to a summary of everything we've talked about here. We hadn't realized we may have something significant to offer because we hadn't really stepped back to see how far we'd come. Their reaction was interesting. First, they were extremely excited about the idea of doing something like we'd done, learning from our hard knocks and reaping the benefits for their business. Usually change management is the most difficult piece of all, so the fact that they were excited and willing so quickly meant they'd won the first several battles in the war before even starting. But then, they had an immediate response of "How can we make this happen?" There's too much, too quickly. They loved the development environment we had created, but trying to understand how they would get from where they were to what we had created was overwhelming. They were almost to the point of giving up when we pointed out that what we created was the result of more than three years of work by a large organization.

The purpose of this final chapter is to get you to be immediately agile and see some quick progress—by figuring out what your first step should be. We share some of our "next steps" as well, and pose some questions that can help determine what the best first steps might be for your specific set of business circumstances.

Figuring Out First Steps

You can't start by trying to do everything; there is just too much. It is important to understand your cost/cycle-time drivers and your value proposition. It is also important to understand the biggest pain points and where you will get the biggest bang for your buck. Then just jump in and start the agile process of learning and evolving. We would suggest starting monthly sprints or MMs, or whatever you would like to call them. Write down some aggressive goals that you think are achievable given all the other work on your plate (see Figure 16.1). Include the other work along with the areas where you would like improvements, including a clear set of priorities. Schedule the checkpoint a month out to see what you accomplished and what you missed. Try to make sure you can include some working demos in your checkpoint so the organization can see the working code coming together. Then review your progress and adjust the objectives for the next checkpoint. It can seem overwhelming if you look at the whole thing. The key is to start the journey and be ready to adjust and learn how to make your organization more productive along the way.

MM1 Objectives

Rank	Theme	Exit Criteria
1		
2		
3		
4		
5		

FIGURE 16.1   Write down your goals

What's Next for FutureSmart?

In reality, we're just about to take our first step, too—our first step toward whatever's next. That's whatever our quest toward improved business results focuses us on that we can accomplish in the next four-week Mini-Milestone/sprint. Maybe we shouldn't have even written this book now. Maybe the real breakthrough from someone in the organization will come next month. And we won't have the chance to write about it. Maybe. But that's the point—it never ends. It's a way of life. The author of a recently written book on large-scale agile recommended it *not* be done unless absolutely necessary. Contrary to that opinion, we've found that large-scale agile just means more opportunities for invention in moving things ahead—more brainpower, more cultural perspective, more pain points to improve. And more scale for being able to afford automated build systems, test farms, and system engineering. It is also more opportunity for camaraderie and meaningful experiences and for coming together as a team that becomes a well-oiled machine.

We are still taking life one sprint at a time. The sidebar "HP FutureSmart Firmware: Our Next 'First Steps'" shows some of the key areas where we are now taking our next first step (the latest pain points we've uncovered). Interestingly, most of these have to do with scaling beyond our 400 people and 10 to 12 products to support and rerelease every quarter. This says that this large-scale agile initiative must be successful if "growing" is our next problem to solve!

HP FutureSmart Firmware: Our Next "First Steps"

- Reducing the time to add a new product to the mix (instantiating a new product in the firmware/tests easily, with autoselection of tests based on links to shared requirements).

- Tools to sparse testing (as we continue to ramp the number of products and features we support, we need to test smarter and automatically sparse testing across platforms and products).

- Synching agile for whole solutions across R&D/ qualification labs. We work with six to eight R&D labs delivering different firmware/software assets, plus a solution test group; most do their own form of agile development, but how do we synch them?

- Agile extended beyond R&D. (Agile is just for firmware/ software, right? What about very nonagile groups that are now impacted as we release faster to the market? Operations/manufacturing, information engineering, customer support, product launch teams—we're helping them challenge 30 years of their waterfall history and they're starting to think outside the box.)

Determining Your First Steps

So where should you start? First, identify your biggest pain points and the value proposition you are striving to accomplish. But then just jump into the sprint or MM process. You don't need a roadmap of every improvement you want to make over the coming months or years. Just take one MM at a time. Get some metrics first. Get some type of autorevert. Get builds/testing happening more often. Remember that to be automated, it's not just autoexecution but autoscheduling of test jobs (completely hands off).

And don't forget to do it your way, based on your business drivers. Here are some fundamental questions to ask yourself as you decide what initiatives should be at the top of your list:

1. Are manual tests a big part of your cost driver and cycle time? You might want to consider starting with test automation as a focus.

2. Are you bringing up a new architecture? You should start by focusing on thin slices and demo of real code in monthly checkpoints.

3. Is monthly/weekly predictability your biggest challenge? Maybe it's okay to start with burndown charts. Or, if you want something more efficient, take a snapshot of what people *think* they can get done as the sprint starts, and compare it to what they actually get done. It takes only two or three sprints for teams to calibrate themselves. And find the right daily metrics to monitor and drive conversations.

4. Is getting your code to meet customer expectations your biggest issue? Start with user stories and test-driven design.

5. Are you having a hard time finishing anything? Consider starting with the lean principle of better controlling your Work in Process (WIP). Make sure you don't let a sprint get interrupted with new requests—those all go into the next sprint.

6. Do you have a consistent bottleneck? Start catering to it.

7. Are you doing big-bang integration? Get an autorevert tool in place with even a simple test suite as a barrier to entry to keep bad code out. Reduce your build time. You want to do anything to make it easy for developers to bring code into the system frequently, in small chunks.

8. Are you spending all your time estimating the future to convince the business that you can deliver? Then scrambling to meet these commitments? Start by investing in system engineers and simple models for long-range prediction. And convince the demand generators that the less you estimate and plan, the more they'll get.

9. Do you have a hard time meeting delivery schedules? Decide up front that a rhythmic release schedule is key, and scope will be what it is. If it doesn't get in now, the next release is soon enough.

10. Are you having a hard time getting your teams engaged and taking ownership for the plans? Maybe you should start with self-managed Scrum teams.

Summary

Whatever your first steps, just remember: Let your people do the talking. Ask engineers from every level in the organization what the biggest pain points are and what needs to improve. You'll find that suddenly any concerns over change management melt away. People become self-invested, and it's not a burden to adopt change. Then have fun taking each step. Learn from it, and become what you want. Large-scale agile is here to stay. And it really does work.

Appendix A

Twelve Principles of Agile Software

Principles Behind the Agile Manifesto

We follow these principles:

Our highest priority is to satisfy the customer
through early and continuous delivery
of valuable software.

Welcome changing requirements, even late in
development. Agile processes harness change for
the customer's competitive advantage.

Deliver working software frequently, from a
couple of weeks to a couple of months, with a
preference to the shorter timescale.

Business people and developers must work
together daily throughout the project.

Build projects around motivated individuals.
Give them the environment and support they need,
and trust them to get the job done.

The most efficient and effective method of
conveying information to and within a development
team is face-to-face conversation.

Working software is the primary measure of progress.

Agile processes promote sustainable development.
The sponsors, developers, and users should be able
to maintain a constant pace indefinitely.

Continuous attention to technical excellence
and good design enhances agility.

Simplicity—the art of maximizing the amount
of work not done—is essential.

The best architectures, requirements, and designs
emerge from self-organizing teams.

At regular intervals, the team reflects on how
to become more effective, then tunes and adjusts
its behavior accordingly.[1]

---

1.   From http://www.agilemanifesto.org/principles.html

BIBLIOGRAPHY

Anderson, David J. *Agile Management for Software Engineering: Applying the Theory of Constraints for Business Results*. Upper Saddle River, NJ: Prentice Hall, 2003.

Cohn, Mike. *User Stories Applied: For Agile Software Development*. Boston, MA: Addison-Wesley, 2004.

Fowler, Martin. "Continuous Integration." 2000. May 1, 2006. <http://martinfowler.com/articles/continuousIntegration.html>

Goldratt, Eliyahu M., and Jeff Cox. *The Goal: A Process of Ongoing Improvement*. Great Barrington, MA: North River Press, 1992.

Highsmith, Jim. "Adaptive Leadership: Accelerating Enterprise Agility." 2011. < http://www.thoughtworks.com/sites/www.thoughtworks.com/files/files/adaptive-leadership-accelerating-enterprise-agility-jim-highsmith-thoughtworks.pdf>

Houndshell, David, and John Smith, Jr. *Based on Science and Corporate Strategy: Du Pont R&D 1902-1980*. New York, NY: Cambridge University Press, 1988.

Humble, Jez, and David Farley. *Continuous Delivery: Reliable Software Releases through Build, Test, and Deployment Automation*. Boston, MA: Addison-Wesley, 2011.

Kennedy, Michael N. *Product Development for the Lean Enterprise: How Toyota's System Is Four Times More Productive and How You Can Implement It*. Richmond, VA: The Oaklea Press, 2003.

Larman, Craig. *Agile & Iterative Development: A Manager's Guide.* Boston, MA: Addison-Wesley, 2004.

Leffingwell, Dean. *Agile Software Requirements: Lean Requirements Practices for Teams, Programs, and the Enterprise.* Boston, MA: Addison-Wesley, 2011.

Leffingwell, Dean. *Scaling Software Agility: Best Practices for Large Enterprises.* Boston, MA: Addison-Wesley, 2007.

Maguire, Steve. *Debugging the Development Process: Practical Strategies for Staying Focused, Hitting Ship Dates, and Building Solid Teams.* Redmond, WA: Microsoft Press, 1994.

Martin, James N. *Systems Engineering Guidebook: A Process for Developing Systems and Products.* Boca Raton, FL: CRC Press, 1997.

Peters, Thomas J., and Robert H. Waterman, Jr. *In Search of Excellence: Lessons from America's Best-Run Companies.* New York, NY: Harper & Row, 1982.

Reinertsen, Donald G. *Managing the Design Factory: A Product Developer's Toolkit.* New York, NY: The Free Press, 1997.

Swartz, James B. *The Hunters and the Hunted: A Non-Linear Solution for Reengineering the Workplace.* Portland, Oregon: Productivity Press, 1994.

INDEX

Symbols

1-N list
    predicting feature delivery, 70-73
    prioritizing, 73

A

Agile and Iterative Management: A Manager's Guide (Larman), 36
agile cycles. *See* mini-milestones (MMs)
agile development, waterfall development versus, 6-8
Agile Manifesto, 2
    principles of, 173-174
agile planning. *See* planning process
agile principles. *See* principles
agile scaling, perspectives on, 159-160
    deployment pipeline changes, 162
    incremental improvements, 164
    team autonomy, 161-162
    uncertainty in planning process, 163-164
Agile Software Requirements: Lean Requirements Practices for Teams, Programs, and the Enterprise (Leffingwell), 155, 160
aligning architecture and business objectives, 17
ALM (Application Lifecycle Management) software, 137-138
architects, role of, 77, 81, 104
architecture. *See also* tools
    aligning with business objectives, 17
        dynamic variability and forward compatibility, 19-22
        existing architecture, challenges with, 18-19
        maintaining architectural integrity, 22-24

re-architecting process
    cultural shifts in, 31-32
    iterative model, 28
    team structure, 28-30
    thin-slice model, 30-31
architecture projects. *See* large innovations
asking questions, permission for, 118-119
automated multilevel testing, 55-61
    on enterprise software systems, 63-65
    L0 testing, 57
    L1 testing, 58
    L2 testing, 58-59
    L3 testing, 59
    L4 testing, 60
    productivity results, 61-63
automated testing
    CTF (Common Test Framework), 131-132
    VMPS (Virtual Machine Provisioning System), 133-136
autonomy of teams, 161-162

B

ballparking high-level initiatives, 70-71
benefits of agile development, 141-142
    developer productivity, 144-146
    product support improvements, 146
    resource usage statistics, 142-144
bottlenecks, 4
    support during, 43
bottom-up change management, top-down versus, 35
building trust, 120
build process, Continuous Integration (CI), 46-54
    on enterprise software systems, 63-65
    productivity results, 61-63